THE ECUMENICAL COUNCIL,
THE CHURCH AND CHRISTENDOM

THE ECUMENICAL COUNCIL,

THE CHURCH AND CHRISTENDOM

by

LORENZ JAEGER
Archbishop of Paderborn

GEOFFREY CHAPMAN
LONDON

This translation of *Das ökumenische Konzil, die Kirche und die Christenheit*, first published by Verlag Bonifacius-Druckerei, Paderborn, in 1960, was made by A. V. Littledale.

© translation, 1961, Geoffrey Chapman Ltd.

PRINTED IN GREAT BRITAIN BY
CHARLES BIRCHALL & SONS LTD.
LIVERPOOL AND LONDON

Contents

Foreword

THE decision of His Holiness, Pope John XXIII, to summon an ecumenical council is the most significant action taken during his pontificate to date. The announcement found an unexpectedly encouraging reception, not only among Catholics, but also among their Orthodox, Protestant, and Anglican brethren. Catholics the world over expect much from the council; indeed, the entire Christian world has taken considerable interest in everything to do with it.

The council's agenda is still unknown. One thing, however, is almost certain : the approaching council will not be a council of reunion, as was the Council of Ferrara-Florence before it which, in 1439, brought about the union of the Greek Orthodox with Rome. It will not be a council convened to discuss with fully authorized representatives of non-Catholic denominations the question of reunion with the Roman Catholic Church. Nevertheless, it is equally certain that Pope John will touch upon matters which lie at the heart of the reunion problem.

This means that the council will be the concern of the Catholic Church and that the affairs of the Church will be dealt with. Pope John made it clear, on April 23, 1959, that the council would do all in its power to meet and answer all claims and demands put upon it by the apostolate. In his letter *Ad Petri cathedram* of June 29, 1959, the following objectives were proposed : the development of the Catholic Faith, the renewal of the Christian life, and the adaptation of ecclesiastical legislation to modern requirements.

At this stage of the preparatory proceedings it is imperative that some thought should be given to the significance of a council, any council, in the life of the Church, for councils are very intimately connected with it. Through them the basic structure of the Church is made known. In January, 1960, during his opening address to the Roman Diocesan Synod, Pope John referred to the twenty previous ecumenical councils, making special mention of the results of the Tridentine and the First Vatican Councils, to which the Church owes its present form.

Though, in the course of the chapters that follow, past councils continually enter the discussion, this is not out of any historical interest, for their historical details have already been treated very thoroughly elsewhere. Our present concern is two-fold : in the first place to make some contribution to a better understanding of what the ecumenical councils can teach us concerning the peculiarities of the Church's constitution, and the continual development of her teaching; then to show the relationship of the councils to "Christendom", the boundaries of which, as far as the first councils were concerned, coincided very closely with those of the Roman Empire and which was in the Middle Ages a structure embracing *Sacerdotium* and *Imperium*. Nowadays the word "Christendom" has acquired a very different meaning, and "Christendom" appears in quite a different aspect. This is all a part of the reunion problem. It should be possible to gain some idea how the coming council could meet its own problems, by examining the previous councils and the way they dealt with their problems.

The fifth chapter links up the "legacy" from the past history of Councils with the "mandate" of the Church and Christianity in the present world. The sixth chapter treats of the extensive preparations for the forthcoming Council, the seventh of the hopes associated with these preparations.

We hope that this work will help towards making the Council

the concern of all Christians. Pope John has spoken of the enthusiastic participation of the people in the early Church Councils, and instanced particularly the case of Ephesus. And today the Press, regardless of its political or religious affiliations, has shown great interest in the Council.

Fifth edition, December, 1960.
LORENZ JAEGER,
Archbishop of Paderborn.

Introduction

Now that the number of ecumenical councils has reached twenty we can look back on them and discern a structure common to them all, and a certain continuity. We cannot, however, remain blind to the fact that the councils change their structure, and that the first eight councils, all of which met in the East, differ considerably from the subsequent councils which met in the West. Further, of the last twelve, the seven medieval councils have a structure differing from the five general councils of the late Middle Ages (first half of the fifteenth century), which in their turn were structurally different from the two sixteenth century councils and the Council of the Vatican.

Three conditioning factors are to be found in these structural variations:

1. Ecclesiology evolves in a manner which has already been defined by Vincent of Lerins (who ascribed the manner of this development to all religious doctrine) in the twenty-third chapter of his *Commonitorium*. Accordingly, the structural form of each council reflects the prevailing ecclesiology and the progressive theological apprehension of the term "Church", that is with regard to its hierarchical structure.

It must be remembered that the Church actively existed before there was any doctrinal teaching as to its precise nature. Christ promised the foundation of the Church and defined its apostolic structure (Matt. 18: 18) under Peter's primacy

(Matt. 16: 19). On Peter he conferred the office of chief Shepherd (John 21: 15-17) and entrusted His mission and the fullness of His power to the apostles (Matt. 28: 18-20) (John 20: 23), whose activity in the early Church (under Peter's guidance) was authoritative, as is shown in the Acts of the Apostles (Acts 15: 28).

While collecting evidence from the first centuries of the primacy of the Bishop of Rome, of the apostolic succession of the bishops, of the unity of the individual episcopal churches, and of the teaching of the bishops and the pope, we must realize that all these aspects existed well before the appearance of any theological concern as to the Church's nature or structure. Theological reflection of this type is closely connected with the life of the Church and is usually occasioned by historical factors. Due to trouble in Corinth, Clement of Rome was moved to intervene and to attest to the apostolic succession. The menace of Gnosis prompted the early development by Ignatius of Antioch, Irenaeus of Lyons and Tertullian of a "theology of the episcopate". The first to appear was not theological doctrine about the Church but about the life of the Church, the proclamation of the Gospel message, the celebration of the holy mysteries, the pastoral care of each community. Theological doctrine is capable of an ever deepening concern with itself, of a continual growth, as the post-Vatican development of ecclesiology has shown. A glance at Pope Pius XII's encyclical *Mystici Corporis* will suffice to show us that ecclesiology even in its most modern guise does not develop independently of the Church's life.

Thus councils were convened before there was any ecclesiological teaching about Councils. The two sources from which such teaching can best be gleaned are the manner in which councils were conducted, and what the participating pope and bishops had to say about them. There is no lack of treatises *de conciliis,* but many questions still remain open and require further investigation. Any attempt at such research would have to be based on the fact that here, where we are concerned with a lasting yet developing basic structure, the form of the councils, as far as Church history and canon law are concerned, is subject to alterations.

2. Equally, a council's form depends upon the prevailing relationship between the Church and its environment, for clearly the Church exists in the actual world, not in a vacuum. As Pope John XXIII emphasized in his inaugural address to the Roman Diocesan Synod, the Church must respond to the changing needs of the times; her very catholicity demands that she is continually aware of, and concerned with, the world's political, social, cultural and economic situations, with which and in which she exists and evolves. Just as what the ecumenical councils have in common, what is lasting in them, reflects the Church's unity, so the change in their form reflects her catholicity. The common factor at the heart of all the councils is their Christ-given basis in the collective action of the apostles and their successors under the guidance of the papacy. Thus each council has its own stamp, and it is possible to group together several councils chosen from one period of history and to see that their form does show signs of consistency.

3. From the beginning synods or councils have appeared as part of the Church's normal organ of governance, but strictly speaking we cannot argue to an absolute necessity for councils —the Pope and bishops need not necessarily have conducted their affairs in conciliar form. For centuries the Church was led, her dogma defined, her liturgy and ecclesiastical structure laid down and binding directions concerning ecclesiastical life issued, without general councils. It was the emperors who were largely responsible for the first general councils; it was at their initiative that the councils were summoned,

though they did make sure of some form of papal agreement.[1]

Nevertheless, it can be maintained that in certain situations the councils were morally necessary to the Church, and that they were, in other respects, of great value, even of decisive importance.

The councils have their prototype in the "Council of Jerusalem". There can be no doubt that under Peter's leadership the apostles as a group gave their advice in important matters that concerned the Church as a whole. It was the "Apostles' Council" that gave judgment on the all-important question arising from the admission of Gentiles into the Church.[2] This was a turning point in the life of the Church. Like the human body the Church grows and gains in strength; she, also, had her teething troubles and for the overcoming of these the councils were without parallel.

One of the Church's first crises occurred at Antioch: "But now some visitors came down from Judaea, who began to tell

---

[1] Rufinus, *Hist, Eccl.* I, 1: Constantine the Great summoned the Council of Nicaea *ex sacerdotum sententia*. For the theological principles of the right to councils, and for the historical problems, cf. J. Forget, "Conciles", in *DAFC*, vol. I (1925), col. 594—599.

[2] Acts 15, 1-25, specially verses 6-7, 22 and 25. For discussions and decisions of the Apostolic College cf. also Acts 6, 1-6. At the opening of the Roman Diocesan Synod on 24th January, 1960, Pope John XXIII pointed to the Council of Jerusalem as being that from which all later councils developed and took their shape, when he said: "Coetus eiusmodi proprio ac definito nomine Concilia appellati sunt. Eorum prima vestigia in libro, qui 'Actus Apostolorum' inscribitur, reperiuntur, quo Concilii Hierosolymitani, ut nuncupatur, memoria traditur, anno quinquagesimo post Christum natum celebrati . . .

"Gravis sane momenti quaestio Apostolos atque seniores Hierosolymas adduxit ad illum primum celebrandum conventum; siquidem iam omnibus prorsus, hebraeis atque ethnicis, aditus ad Ecclesiam patebat: quaerebatur igitur an circumcisio ceteraque Mosaicae Legis praescripta hebraeis adhuc servanda essent, et ethnicos quoque antiquis illis ritibus obstringi necesse esset, si re atque nomine christiani fieri vellent, quo quidem nomine Christi asseclae Antiochiae iam appellari solebant."

After the Pope has outlined the discussions and decisions of the Council he goes on to the first ecumenical council which was summoned three hundred years later, draws attention to the Arian dispute and continues: "Hinc opportunitas generales conventus convocandi, quibus quidem, instar Hierosolymitani Concilii, Petri successor praeesset ac moderaretur; seniores autem cum eo quaestiones excutiendo atque diiudicando adiutricem praestarent operam." *AAS*, vol. LII (1960), pp. 180-182.

the brethren, You cannot be saved without being circumcised according to the tradition of Moses." (Acts 15 : 1). Consequently "it was decided that Paul and Barnabas and certain of the rest should go up to see the apostles and presbyters in Jerusalem about this question. . . . When they reached Jerusalem, they were welcomed by the church, and by the apostles and presbyters; and they told them of all that God had done to aid them. But some believers who belonged to the party of the pharisees came forward and declared, They must be circumcised; we must call upon them to keep the law of Moses." (Acts 15 : 2-5).

The heated arguments were endangering the Church's missionary activity and threatened the Christian doctrine of justification. A clear and final ruling was needed. Therefore "the apostles and presbyters assembled to decide about this matter" (Acts 15 : 6). This second assembly is rightly called the "Council of the Apostles". Along with the apostles "the presbyters" also took part; the latter were not apostles yet they had a rank which distinguished them from the community at large. Judas Barsabas and Silas probably belonged to the "apostolic circle" for they are described as "leading men among the brethren" (Acts 15 : 22). They received their authority from the apostles through an act of consecration, "through the imposition of hands", and also they were called bishops : "The Holy Spirit has made you bishops; you are to be the shepherds of that flock . . ." (Acts 20 : 28).

The assembly was the scene of lively discussions. Finally, Peter rose and referred to the office to which God had called him; how the Gentiles were to hear the gospel message from his lips and so embrace the faith. He recalled to the assembly the decision he had reached when he received the Gentile, Cornelius, into the Church. As then, so here, Peter's word was final : his authority and his arguments silenced all opposition. After Paul and Barnabas had described the miracles that God had worked to strengthen their preaching among the Gentiles, James expressed fundamental agreement with Peter's statements and proposed that neither circumcision nor the law should be imposed on the Gentiles but that the Gentile Christians should be careful not to offend Jewish-Christian sensibilities. The apostles and presbyters ratified this proposal. That this decision is to be regarded as a solemn article of faith is clear when it is remembered that "some believers" had wished to make observance of the law of Moses necessary for salvation. On the other hand, the clauses relating to abstinence "from meat which has been strangled or has blood on it" added to the decree at James' suggestion, were of a disciplinary nature; this can be seen clearly from the motives behind James' proposal and from the decree's closing words. It is noteworthy that Luke considered the council's decision final; the question was solved.

In the middle of the second century, synods comprising Asian bishops met to suppress Montanism.[3] A few decades later episcopal synods met at the wish of Pope Victor "in Palestine, Asia, Pontus, Gaul and in Rome"[4] to handle the conflict over the feast of Easter. Two significant synods met in Antioch in the years 264 and 268 and condemned Paul of Samosata's heretical teaching. The second of these synods, at which seventy bishops were present, informed the Bishop of Rome, the Bishop of Alexandria and every bishop in Christendom of its findings, thus showing that the synod, though provincial, was aware of its link with "the whole Catholic Church on earth".[5]

As from the third century, provincial synods in Asia Minor, in Africa (Carthage) and in Italy (Rome), became regular features of Church life. No longer provincial in character, the Synod of Arles which met in 314 at Emperor Constantine's

---

[3]Eusebius, *Hist. Eccl.* V, 16, 10.
[4]*ibid.* V, 23; V, 24, 8.
[5]*ibid.* VII, 30, 2.

instigation, was attended by forty-seven bishops who represented virtually the whole of the Western Church. It was Constantine's hope that the unanimous judgment of the assembled bishops would put an end to the Donatist controversy and the unrest this heresy was causing.[6]

Similarly, in 325, fifty-six bishops from Palestine, Syria, Arabia, Phoenicia and Cappadocia met in Antioch to condemn the Arian heresies and to formulate the traditional Christian faith.

[6]*ibid*. X, 5, 23-24.

CHAPTER ONE

The First Eight Ecumenical Councils and their Ecclesiology

I T is reasonable to suppose that the two synods of 314 and 325 gave Constantine the idea of assembling in an "ecumenical council" every bishop of his empire, with the purpose of killing Arianism. Clearly such an assembly would not be possible until after the persecutions had come to an end.

I

Emperor and Council

In his empire, to which he had brought peace and unity, Constantine the Great possessed both the authority and the material means to assemble the bishops, even those who were hesitant or reluctant. He wrote "very respectful" letters inviting them first to Ancyra and then to Nicea, and at the same time placed at their disposal the imperial postal service (the *cursus publicus*) for their journeys, and his palace in Nicea for the assembly. The resulting Council of Nicea, in Bithynia, which opened on 20th May, 325, with almost three hundred bishops present, most of them Eastern,[1] was the first

---

[1] By tradition the number of bishops was 318; cf. Gen. 14, 14.

ecumenical council. Its order of procedure was similar to that of the Roman Senate. Pope Sylvester sent two Roman priests as legates and probably Bishop Hosius of Cordoba presided. Hosius, perhaps the emperor's theological adviser during the proceedings, was the first to sign the decrees; the Pope's two representatives followed and after them the other bishops.

The emperor was alive to his obligations as the protector of the Church's peace and unity. He was not only the Church's guardian and champion, but also, as the Eastern Church described him, he was "equal with, and similar to, an apostle", the *episcopus ab externo*, as he called himself.[2] These titles were not merely rhetorical. They had a theological and political significance and in assuming them Constantine acknowledged a duty received from God. Everyone in the empire, Christian and heathen alike, was subject to him in his role of overlord. His calling was to lead Gentiles and heretics to the true Faith and to encourage Christians to persist in the practice of their beliefs. The Emperor, as supervisor of the political community, was Christ's representative just as the bishops, as supervisors of the ecclesiastical communities, were Christ's representatives. But to the political gamut were added duties which came to the emperor from the religious and ecclesiastical sphere. Constantine said of himself : "God has selected my office for the fulfilment of his plans, . . . so that I, entrusted with higher power, might disperse prevailing dangers, and so that mankind, through my assistance, might return to the service of the most holy law and that the most sacred faith, under the powerful leadership of the Almighty, might win more souls to its side."[3] Therefore, "the emperor confirmed the decision proclaimed at

---

[2]Eusebius, *Vita Constantini* IV 24. Cf. for the following: J. Straub, "Kaiser Konstantin als, ἐπίσκοπος τῶν ἐκτός " in *Studia Patristica*, vol. I, Berlin 1957, pp. 678-695.

[3]Eusebius, *Vita Constantini*, II, 28.

episcopal synods; and the provincial governors were forbidden to hinder their application, for the priest of God ranked higher than any judge".[4]

Even if this justification of his attitude by virtue of rank were merely a statement of Eusebius' own opinion, nonetheless "the fact that the council's decrees could be declared binding by imperial law remains incontestable; this means that in this case the civil authorities could institute legal proceedings against Christian subjects who disregarded the Council's decrees. We are still a long way from the eventual foundation of the State-Church (under Theodosius) but the beginnings of this development are already visible".[5]

The emperor felt himself pledged to the whole of Christendom. "When he heard that numerous Churches had been established among the Persians and that countless believers had joined Christ's flock, he rejoiced at this news as though the concerns of all peoples were his to carry, and he extended his all-embracing solicitude to this country as well."[6]

Constantine recommended these Christians to the protection of the Persian monarch. Eusebius said "that henceforth all peoples of the earth were directed by one pilot and they rejoiced in their life under the servant of God.[7]

Christendom's mission was a universal one and so was the Christian emperor's. The Christendom of the first millennium was experiencing its formative years; its emperor, its secular leader, considered himself in his sacred role of supervisor comparable to a bishop. But Constantine was still uncertain as to the nature of his place inside the Church, and this was one of the reasons why he postponed baptism until the end of his life.[8]

---

[4]*ibid.* IV, 27.
[5]J. Straub, in: *Studia Patristica*, vol. I, Berlin 1957, p. 684, n.1.
[6]Eusebius, *Vita Constantini*, IV, 8.
[7]*ibid.* IV, 14.
[8]J. Straub, *loc. cit.* pp. 686-687.

Eusebius said that Constantine convoked the Church assemblies "as if God had set him up as Bishop of all bishops".[9] Did Constantine ever assume the title of an *episcopus episcoporum?* We know that Bishop Lucifer of Cagliari vigorously rejected this title when Constantine II (d. 361) usurped it: *Tu qui es profanus ad Dei domesticos quare tibi sumis Dei sacerdotum auctoritatem?* Why do you, who are of the secular order as compared with God's servants, usurp the authority of God's priests?[10] Constantine was not *profanus* only because he was a heretic but because even the orthodox emperor belongs to the secular domain as distinct from divine episcopal authority, even though God has bestowed upon him a sacred *sublimitas regalis.* It was here that there arose for the first time the problem of differentiating between the civil and ecclesiastical domains. Eusebius, in comparing the emperor with the bishop of all bishops, is still struggling for a solution. "However, Constantine's own actions at the council of Nicea throw the distinction between the two domains in clear perspective. Eusebius could not address him, *proprio sensu,* as bishop, let alone as 'pope'. It is clear from the detailed description of the Council of Nicea that Constantine arranged for a bishop to preside and that he himself did not have a vote. However, it did lie within his power and judgment to have the decrees made law."[11] In a letter to the Church at Alexandria, Constantine rejoiced in the victory at Nicea: "In overcoming the controversies, divisions and confusion, the splendour of truth has conquered the lethal poisons of difference of opinion, and it has been done according to God's will." He went on to state the theological basis for the authority of the Council's decrees: "The agreement of the three hundred bishops is nothing other than the decision of God".[12]

---

[9]Eusebius, *Vita Constantini*, I, 44.
[10]Lucifer of Calaris, *De Sancto Athanasio*, I, 7.
[11]J. Straub, *loc. cit.*, p. 692.
[12]Socrates, *Historia Ecclesiae*, I, 9.

The historico-theological aspects which St Augustine pointed out in his praise of the Christian Emperor, and which his disciple Orosius treated more fully, found a degree of fulfilment in Constantine's conception of "empire" which was to have a considerable influence on future history.[13] It is in this light that Constantine's actions are to be understood : his summoning of the bishops to the Council; his proclamation of the Council's decrees, which he also invested with a civil application, as imperial law; and his action in exiling those bishops excommunicated by the Council. The emperors Constantine, Theodosius, Marcian and Justinian wished merely to do their duty as sovereigns of the empire.

II

The Popes and the First Ecumenical Councils

Broadly speaking, the part played by the popes in the convocation of a council was that of recognizing the convocation's legitimacy by sending their representatives to the council.[14] Further generalization is impossible, as the extent of their closer participation varied. After the Council of Chalcedon, Pope Leo the Great wrote that the General Council was "convoked by the emperor with the approval of the Apostolic Chair".[15]

---

[13]P. Brezzi, "Una 'civitas terrena spiritualis' come ideale storico-politico di Sant' Agostino," in: *Augustinus Magister*, Vol. I, Paris 1954, pp. 915-922; St Augustine, *De civ. Dei*, V, 24-26; Orosius, *Historia adversus paganos*; R. Janin, "L'empéreur dans l'Eglise byzantine," in *Nouv. Revue Théol.*, Vol. 77, 1955, pp. 49-60; J. Vogt, "Constantinus der Grosse," in: *RAC*, Vol. III, Stuttgart 1957, pp. 307-379; for the Council of Nicea: *ibid*. pp. 338-343; Bibliography: *ibid*. pp. 378-379.

[14]Cf. Pope Celestine, *Ep*. 19, 1; Leo the Great, *Ep*. 93, 1.

[15]*Ep*. 114, 1; for the whole, cf. J. Forget, *loc. cit*., col. 594-607: "Convocation, présidence, confirmation des conciles oecuméniques".

Generally, a council's decrees were confirmed by the pope by being signed by his representatives in his name. There was no dichotomy between pope and council. The latter met in union with the pope who was united with his bishops by virtue of his office as St Peter's successor. The pope actually participated through his legates.

Just before the Council of Ephesus, Pope Celestine wrote to Emperor Theodosius II: "At the Council, which will meet at your request, our presence will be shown by the attendance of our legates."[16] Leo the Great appealed to established custom in not appearing personally at the Council of Chalcedon; he would not be missed, he said, for he would be present in his representatives.[17]

In this way pope and council acted together. Speaking in Pope Celestine's name, the Roman priest Philippus told the Council Fathers at Ephesus: "The members have united themselves with the head, for your Graces are well aware that the holy Apostle Peter is the Faith and the Head of the Apostles."[18]

---

[16]*Ep.* 19, 1.

[17]*Ep.* 93, 1.

[18]At the Council of Chalcedon the bishops asked Pope Leo the Great for a formal confirmation of the disciplinary regulations which had been drawn up in the absence of the papal legates. Leo claimed the right to declare Canon 28 invalid. When Leo confirmed the acts of the council he attested once again his complete accordance with the council in matters of faith. Nonetheless a formal juridical act was not necessary for those regulations which had been drawn up and signed with his representatives' collaboration. If the emperor now, as after the later councils (2nd and 3rd councils of Constantinople) sought confirmation from the pope, this confirmation was intended as a solemn declaration of the agreement of the pope and the bishops of the West, in which the pope's assent assumed decisive significance.

III

The Eastern Church and the First Seven Ecumenical Councils

The first eight ecumenical councils—all convoked by the reigning emperors and all meeting in the East at Nicea, Constantinople, Ephesus and Chalcedon—constitute the first group of the general Church assemblies. Of this group the first four stand out prominently: Pope Gregory the Great expressed for them the same reverence as he expressed for the four Gospels. These first four councils formulated Trinitarian and Christological dogma and in so doing firmly secured the foundations of Christendom.

The Orthodox Churches, separated from Rome since 1054, recognize the first seven councils as ecumenical. Indeed, these Churches refer to themselves as the "Churches of the Seven Councils". In their view, the infallible decisions of the first seven councils should be the basic criteria upon which all the subsequent councils should base their findings. The Orthodox theologian, George Racoveanu, has written: "If throughout the first eight centuries infallibility characterized the ecumenical council, then for the centuries that followed, the years of schism, infallibility must imply agreement. It cannot be maintained that the properties that make a council "ecumenical" vanished after 787 (Second Council of Nicea) or 1054, for that would mean that the Holy Spirit was no longer present in Christ's Church, that he had ceased to operate in her. Life continually poses problems which it is the Church's duty to solve. But the Church has no problems that lack some sort of connection with those that faced the first seven councils, or with those other problems solved by the Church's leaders. From apostolic times onwards all difficulties were clarified, if not according to the letter of the law, then certainly according to its spirit. Therefore, the criterion by which post-787 councils must be judged as ecumenical is the extent to which their decisions in matters of faith or morals agree with the decisions reached by the seven ecumenical councils. Should an unexpected problem arise to which a present-day council found a solution, one that did not contradict the spirit of ecumenical dogma but that showed this dogma in a yet clearer form, such a decision would be considered by the bishops to be an enrichment of already existing dogma.[19]

The first seven ecumenical councils were those of Nicea in 325, Constantinople in 381, Ephesus in 431, Chalcedon in 451, the Second Council of Constantinople in 553, the Third Council of Constantinople in 680 and the Second Council of Nicea in 787. The "Council of Images" of 787 was concerned with the meaning and lawfulness of the veneration of images: God became man, therefore he may be portrayed as a man, and icons of him, his mother, and of the angels and saints may be venerated. The theological labour of the Eastern Church was completed. The institution on 11th March, 843, of the "Feast of Orthodoxy" in lasting memory of the restoration of the veneration of images, saw the birth of the *orthodox* "Church of the Seven Councils". From now on the East took very little part in the problems which were to bother the Western Church, just as formerly, when Pelagianism was rampant in the West, the East had remained virtually unaffected. The manner in

---

[19]G. Racoveanu, "L'Oecumenicité, Point de vue de l'Orthodoxie roumaine," in: *Lumière et Vie*, vol. VIII (1959) No. 45, p. 143. In our view the last thirteen ecumenical councils have the same infallibility as the first seven. Cf. J. N. Karmiris, "Outline of the dogmatic teaching of the orthodox catholic Church", in: *The Greek View of the Orthodox Church*, ed. by Panagiotis Bratsiotis, Stuttgart 1959, pp. 85-100; B. Schultze S.J., "Das Unionskonzil von Florenz," in: *Stimmen der Zeit*, Vol. 164 (1958/59), pp. 427-439.

which Western reformers formulated their questions remained alien to the Eastern Church. This was a result not only of the Great Schism of 1054, but far more of a particular type of theological reasoning. The two theological systems of East and West would benefit considerably from a free exchange of ideas (and this does sometimes happen); by this means Western theology can, and does, gain in energy, scope and fruitfulness.[20]

The last ecumenical council of the first millennium also took place in Constantinople, meeting from 869-70. At this council the unity of the Eastern and Western Churches received vigorous emphasis, the schism of Patriarch Photius was terminated and the primacy of the pope was recognised.[21] But the deep-seated estrangement between East and West continued. The linguistic, cultural and political cleavage paved the way for the disastrous division that would never have arisen had varying methods of theological reasoning been the only causes of friction.[22]

IV

The Ecclesiology of the Ecumenical Councils in the First Millennium

The ecclesiology of the first ecumenical councils can be gleaned from their decrees, from the letters of those

---

[20]Cf. G. Dejaifve, S.J., "Orient et Occident chrétien: deux théologies?" in: *Nouvelle Revue Théologique*, vol. 92 (1960), pp. 3-19; B. Schultze S.J., "Problemi di teologia presso gli ortodossi—Spirito genuino dell 'ortodossia," in: *Orient. Christ. Period.*, vol. VII (1941), pp. 149-205; J. Brinktrine, "Das Ökumenische Konzil und die Orthodoxen," in: *Theologie und Glaube*, vol. 49 (1959), pp. 241-256.
[21]Denz. 336-341.
[22]W. de Vries, *Der christliche Osten in Geschichte und Gegenwart*, Würzburg 1951, pp. 72-76.

participating, from contemporary theological writings inspired by the councils and questions arising in them, and particularly from the wording of the decisions on questions of doctrine and discipline reached in these councils. The following four points stand out prominently from these sources:[23]

1. The ecumenical council was an assembly of bishops representing the entire Church. The presence of papal representatives guaranteed the unity of the Eastern and Western Churches. The number and origins of the participating bishops were not without meaning for the representation of the whole Church, but neither were they crucial. Even if the number of participants was small and they all came from the East, a council could still represent the whole Church in that it conducted its affairs in "syntaxis with the head", in unison with St Peter's successor, as those at Chalcedon said. There, at Chalcedon, explicit recognition of papal authority reached its zenith. It was an authority established not only through the powerful spiritual personality of Leo the Great but also through the evolution of a clearer understanding of the papal office.

2. The assembled bishops negotiated as successors of the apostles and in unison with the successor of St Peter. Eusebius compared the councillors at Nicea with the "Choir of Apostles", and Pope Celestine attached the same significance to the assembly of bishops at Ephesus as he did to the Apostles' Council at Jerusalem (Acts 15). He called to mind the apostles Paul and John and urged: "We must preserve what we have inherited from apostolic succession".[24] Athanasius wrote that they ought to "adhere to their apostolic foundation and keep a firm hold on the faith of the fathers".[25] They believed that through apostolic succession Christ was with his bishops and this belief was symbolized at Ephesus by a throne containing a

---

[23]Taken from P. Th. Camelot, "Les conciles oecuméniques dans l'Antiquité in: Lumière et Vie, loc. cit., pp. 12-17; cf. J. Forget, loc. cit., col. 596-612.
[24]Ep. 18.
[25]De synodis, 54.

book of the gospels which was placed in the middle of the basilica in which the Council took place. Those at Chalcedon and at the Third Council of Constantinople regarded Christ's promise to be in the midst of people assembled in his name as an assurance of his support for the Council.

3. The fathers of the councils were the bearers and representatives of tradition and the rightful expounders of Holy Scriptures. Their unanimous agreement proclaimed the Church's faith. Through reasoning based on Holy Scripture, the Council of Nicea established the meaning of "consubstantial". Athanasius said: "This is the faith given to us by Christ, preached by the apostles and delivered to us by the councillors at Nicea who came from all parts of the Church".[26] Those at the Second Council recognized "what is handed down to us by Holy Scripture as well as the traditions of the Fathers and the definitions of that same Faith made by the said four councils".[27] The Council's decrees proclaim the faith of the whole Church, as this faith is contained in Scripture and Tradition.

4. Because of the presence of the Holy Spirit, promised to the Church by Christ, the councils' decisions were infallible. Pope Celestine wrote to the Council of Ephesus: "The assembly of bishops testifies to the presence of the Holy Spirit".[28] Leo the Great described the decrees of Nicea and Chalcedon as the work of the Holy Spirit, for they were arrived at "through the guidance of the Holy Spirit".[29] Consequently

---

[26]*Ad Afros* 1; cf. *ibid.* 4: The fathers of the Council "breathe Holy Scripture"; *De synodis,* 5: The fathers of Nicea have nothing new, only the teaching of the apostles, similarly in *De decr. Nic. syn.,* 3.

[27]Denz 228. The Synod of Antioch, which condemned Arianism at the beginning of 325 (cf. above p. xvii) imparted its resolutions to all other bishops of the whole Church and especially to the Bishop of Rome and with him the bishops of Italy, who accepted the decrees of the synod and formally confirmed them. In this way the faith of the whole Church took expression in a declaration of doctrine which can be considered as a preliminary to the ecumenical council of Nicea.

[28]*Ep.* 18, 1: *Spiritus Sancti testatur praesentiam congregatio sacerdotum.*

[29]*Ep.* 104, 3: *instruente Spiritu Sancto.*

an ecumenical council's decrees have universal, permanent validity.

These points constitute the main features of conciliar ecclesiology, and they apply to all ecumenical, ecclesiastical assemblies. During the Vatican Council, Fr. Joseph Kleutgen S.J. devised for the *Deputatio de Fide* the "scheme of a second dogmatic constitution concerning the Church of Christ", which was finally left undiscussed. Concerning the theological foundation and authority of ecumenical councils it was said in this scheme : Illud enim ligandi et solvendi pontificium, quod Petro soli datum est, collegio quoque apostolorum, suo tamen capiti coniuncto, tributum esse constat, protestante Domino (Matt. 18 : 8) ... Quapropter inde ab ecclesiae primordiis oecumenicorum conciliorum decreta et statuta iure merito tanquam Dei sententiae et Spiritus sancti placita summa veneratione et pari obsequio a fidelibus suscepta sunt".[30]

[30]Mansi, *Sacrorum conciliorum nova et amplissima collectio*, Vol. 53, col. 310– For the authority of ecumenical councils and the relation of the pope to the bishops assembled in council cf. M. Goemans O.F.M., " Chalcedon as 'General Council'," in : *The Council of Chalcedon*, ed. by A. Grillmeier S.J. and H. Bacht, S.J., Vol. I, Würzburg 1951, pp. 251-289; Hugo Rahner, S.J "Leo der Grosse, der Papst des Konzils," *ibid*. pp. 323-339.—M. Goeman declares: "Even if we find in regard to the convocation and procedure of general council in the fifth century the same basic ideas as in the centur before, there is nonetheless a step forward to be noticed in the recognition the pope's right to lay down the agenda of a general council and to contr its proceedings. The same must be said of the understanding about th necessity for the pope's complete ratification of the council's decrees." (*loc. c* pp. 289).

CHAPTER TWO

The Seven Councils of the Middle Ages, their Particular Form and Ecclesiological Peculiarity

T HE world had altered considerably by the time of the first three Lateran Councils, 1123, 1139 and 1179. Schism had cut off the Eastern Churches. When in 1123 Pope Calixtus II convoked the First Lateran Council in Rome, the Byzantine Church was not represented at all, as for the last sixty-nine years the Patriarch of Constantinople and the bishops of the Byzantine Empire were no longer in communion with the Pope. A whole century of cultural and political estrangement had preceded the events of the summer of 1054, culminating on 16th July, 1054, when the Cardinal Legate, Humbert, placed a Papal Bull on the altar in Constantinople's *Hagia Sophia* excommunicating Patriarch Michael Caerularius.

I

Sacerdotium and Imperium

Charles the Great's coronation as Emperor at the hands of Pope Leo III was undoubtedly one of the main causes underlying the mounting dislike that the East had for the

"Latins". Up till now the Roman Empire had included (if only theoretically) both Eastern and Western Christendom. Since the end of the West Roman Empire in 476 there had been only one emperor of all these territories, and he had reigned from Constantinople. The kings of the German Empires, whose territories formerly constituted the West Roman Empire, received from the emperor in Constantinople the title "Consul", or some other honorary title, which served to connect them to the empire. But East Rome would never give them the respect due exclusively to the *Basileus* (King).

The Lombard menace, and Constantinople's inability to come to Rome's aid, led in the eighth century to the pope's turning to Gaul for help. When Pope Zachary in 751 acknowledged Pepin as king, and when Pope Stephen II arranged with Pepin that the *respublica romana* should become the *Patrimonium Petri* and accorded the Frankish king the title of a *Patricius Romanus*, a development began which subsequently reached its zenith at the coronation of Charles the Great as Emperor on Christmas Day of the year 800. Although this coronation was probably discussed in Paderborn (799) at the meeting between pope and emperor, Charles' astonishment and hesitation on the matter is understandable. The acclamations of the Roman people who greeted him as Augustus gave him some conception of the momentousness of the approaching historical change. It must be remembered that according to the Byzantine viewpoint the pope could bestow neither the title of *Patricius Romanus* nor the title of emperor, and that Byzantium regarded the *respublica romana* theoretically as still the pope's principal concern.[1] Making a "barbarian

---

[1] It would appear that, in order to justify the existence of the new West Roman Empire, the theory of the Donatio Constantini was put forward between 802 and 812 by a cleric of St Denis. Cf. E. Griffe, "Aux origines de l'état pontificale," in: *Bulletin de littérature ecclésiastique*, Vol. 53 (1952), pp. 216-231; Vol. 55 (1954), pp. 65-89; Vol. 59 (1958), pp. 193-211; Vol. 58 (1957), pp. 238-241: "A propos de la Donatio Constantini."—The *Donatio Constantini*, which is based on a forgery, is difficult to distinguish from the *Translatio Imperii*, which is historically authenticated.

king" emperor was felt by the Byzantines to be not only an assault on their rights but also the destruction of the unity of the Christian Universal Empire, whose boundaries coincided virtually with those of Christendom and which was founded by Constantine the Great.

The Romans, acclaiming Charles the Great, had shouted "To Carolus Augustus, crowned by God, the mighty and peace-bringing Emperor, life and victory!" But they were thinking of their small West Roman Empire, with the *Patrimonium Petri*. Neither the Romans nor Charles the Great wanted what would amount to a continuation of the old Imperium Romanum, and both recognized the existence of two empires, the Byzantine and the Carlovingian.[2] It was not until the close of the ninth century that the idea of a papal "assumption of the imperial power" (for the greater security of the Church) was clearly put forward.[3]

However, the decisive step in the disengagement of the West from the Byzantine Empire, had been taken. The Carlovingian Empire was developing the machinery and conditions that were to favour the medieval Imperium (already in embryonic form) with its part-religious, part-secular culture and its constricted Church-State symbiosis.

In 936, Otto the Great had himself crowned in Aachen on Charles the Great's throne. This action formed a symbolic link between his own conception of "empire" and Carlovingian tradition. When, in 962, he was crowned emperor in Rome by Pope John XII, he brought about a renewal of the western empire and took upon himself the duty of protecting the Church as well as that of keeping a watchful eye on the unity of Christendom. It is true that he recognized the Byzantine ruler as the East Roman Emperor and even arranged the

[2] Cf. W. Ohnsorge, *Das Zweikaiserproblem im frühen Mittelalter*, Hildesheim 1947.
[3] P. A. van den Baar, *Die kirchliche Lehre von der Translatio Imperii Romani* (*Analecta Gregoriana* 78), Rome 1956, p. 16.

15

marriage of his son, Otto II, to the Byzantine Princess Theophano, but the old conception of the universal Roman Empire had been revived and led now to the total victory of the conviction that the western emperor was the legitimate successor of the Roman Caesars and Constantine the Great.

The Empire of the Ottos had a marked spiritual and ecclesiastical character. The *Imperium Christianum* became synonymous with the *Imperium Romanum*. Just as there was only one Christendom, so it became increasingly impossible to conceive of more than one Christian Empire and one Emperor.[4] Due to this spiritual interpretation of the Imperium the idea of papal assumption of the empire could evolve unharassed. The relationship between *Sacerdotium* and *Imperium* established then was to decide the future turn of events and became the main theme in the councils of the central period of the Middle Ages.

II

The Conflict over Investitures and the First Three Lateran Councils

In spite of the brevity of Otto III's rule (983-1002), his conception of the universal Roman Empire had a considerable influence on future policy and survived throughout the Middle Ages. Henry II (1002-24) and Henry III (1039-56), conscious of their sacred office and mission, encouraged Cluny's reform movement, which put fresh life into the Church and led to a strengthening of papal authority.

The Empire's predominance was most noticeable at the

---

[4] P. E. Schramm, *Kaiser, Rom und Renovatio*, 2nd impr., Darmstadt 1957.

Synod of Sutri (1046). It would seem that the Western Emperor's power over the Church was similar to that wielded by the *Basileus* in Constantinople. The *Privilegium Ottonianum* of 13th February, 962, had already laid down that the Pope, even after canonical election, could not be crowned until he had sworn fidelity to the emperor. After the insurrection of 963, the Romans had had to swear on oath never to elect a pope who did not have the emperor's approval. The Ottonians and the early Salians understood their empire as a type of patriarchal sovereign authority combining Church and State in the one Christendom at the head of which stood the emperor. The bishops, as well as the pope, were to be fitted into the combination of Church and Empire.[5] More so than the Ottonians, the Salian Emperors realized the ambiguity of this situation: the empire ruled the Church but a dependent and degraded Church could never offer the empire strong support. Consequently the first Salians supported the reform movement and encouraged the first reform popes. The work of reform, borne in the main by Cluny, made the *Libertas Ecclesiae* the main demand in their programme. As from Leo IX's pontificate (1048-54), the papacy triumphantly evaded imperial control, renewed the dignity and supremacy of the *Sacerdotium* and insisted upon the independence of the Church in her relationship with the State. Facing the reform popes was the sticky problem of removing the bishops from the emperor's power without thereby undermining the empire. The bishops were at once the empire's ecclesiastical pastors and its feudal tenants; this was where the difficulty lay. The conflict over investitures,

---

[5]L. Santifaller, "Zur Geschichte des ottonisch-salischen Reichskirchensystems," *Sitzungsberichte der Österreichischen Akademie der Wissenschaften* 229, 1, Vienna 1954, p. 14: The ecclesiastical system of the empire had developed since Merovingian times from the union of the universal Christian religion with the Roman concept of empire and the nature of the native Germanic church. These three elements—the Germanic comprises an element both of public and of private law—gave shape to the Kingdom of the Frankish Nation, whose political and theological foundation was taken over by the Ottonians and the Salians.

which reached its climax under Gregory VII and Henry IV and its conclusion in the Worms Concordat (1122), was a result of all this. The bishops continued to be feudal tenants of the empire but were invested, in Germany, after ecclesiastical election and before consecration with the mace—no longer with ring and crozier—and in Italy and Burgundy not until after election and consecration.

The conflict was overcome. The fact that bishops, abbots and priests received their spiritual faculties from God and the representatives of the Church, and that it was the duty of these dignitaries to protect the Church's interests, had been stressed. The Church's freedom had been saved—a new era had begun. It was natural, therefore, that Pope Calixtus II should convoke one year later a council to be held at the Lateran which would ratify the Worms Concordat. We have no records of the proceedings at this, the first council of the Middle Ages. The Council's canons regulated the administration of the sacraments, prohibited simony and ordination by anti-popes or by bishops whose office was invalid. They endorsed the truce of God proclaimed at Clermont. The canons were also concerned with a number of topics, the nature of which was more social than religious.

The first Lateran Council was "already to a large extent the rendezvous and the forum of Christendom".[6] This description is even more valid of the second Lateran Council which lasted from 4th April, 1139, until the end of the month. Those taking part came from every Christian country in the world. The reason for calling the council was the schism of the anti-pope, Anacletus II, whose disciples were deposed. Most of the thirty canons carried Gregory VII's reforms a stage further. Canon 23 is important for its excommunication of sectaries who rejected "the Eucharist, infant Baptism, the priesthood and

---

[6]H. Jedin, *Ecumenical Councils in the Catholic Church, an historical survey*, Herder/Nelson, 1960.

marriage". There showed themselves at this time the first signs of those heretical sects, such as the Cathari, which threatened the stability of the medieval Church-State. The conciliar decrees bit deep into the social and cultural life of the times.

The conflict over investitures and the schism had determined the turn of events leading up to the first two Lateran Councils. A bitter quarrel over the relationship between the *Sacerdotium* and *Imperium* and over the schism of the antipopes, Victor IV, Paschal III and Calixtus III, terminated in the Peace of Venice, 1177, which foresaw the Third Lateran Council convoked by Alexander III in 1179. This council set the Church's seal on the Peace of Venice, "by which the ascendancy of the pope was further consolidated. 'The council,' the pope said in his invitation to the bishops of Tuscany, 'acting in conformity with the custom of the Fathers' would confirm the peace and impart to it an authority which it would not otherwise possess. Thus Alexander is already linking up with the councils of the early Church".[7] His plan was to gather round him the whole Christian world. Apart from about three hundred bishops from the countries of Europe and from the States founded by the Crusaders, a great number of abbots and "the ambassadors of almost all the emperors, kings and princes of the whole of Christendom were present".[8]

The third Lateran Council presents even more clearly than its two predecessors the specifically medieval type of general council. It represents not only the Church but also the *civitas christiana*, God's State on earth. The pope conducted the proceedings in person; and, as in the councils of the first millennium, the bishops are by divine right enfranchised participators in the council. But quite apart from the bishops, the pope assembled a large number of abbots and superiors of religious orders, in order to discuss their affairs with them. These people

[7]H. Jedin, *loc. cit.*
[8]*ibid.*

participated in the council by ecclesiastical right. This distinction plays an important part in the councils' structural change, and it is still valid today. In addition, the pope assembled the Christian princes to discuss with them, for instance, the crusades, social questions and the safeguarding of the Faith.

III

The Fourth Lateran Council as Presentation of the Christianity of the Central Period of the Middle Ages

On 19th April, 1213, Pope Innocent III convoked the Fourth Lateran Council "in accordance with the practice of the ancient fathers", and on 11th November, 1215, he opened the council. He had invited the Eastern and Western bishops, the superiors of the monastic orders, the representatives of the cathedral chapters, and also all Christian monarchs. The Greek Orthodox bishops of the Patriarchate of Constantinople, although invited to the council, were not present among the four hundred and twelve other participating bishops. Otherwise, from Esthonia, Lithuania and Poland to Portugal, from England to the remote East, the whole of Christianity was represented by its bishops and by Emperor Frederick II, by the kings of France, England, Aragon and Hungary, and by representatives of the crusader states and of a few cities. The judgments made were directed against the Cathari, against Berengarius of Tours' interpretation of the Eucharist and against Joachim de Fiore's teaching on the Trinity.[9] Chapter 21 obliged every Christian who had reached the age of reason to receive the sacraments of Penance and the Eucharist at least once a year. The Council's far-reaching reform legislation became, for the

---

[9]Denz 428-434.

most part, canon law. The proceedings against the heresies differed in procedure from that of the very early Church in that the heresies, as underground movements, were regarded not only as against the faith but also as detrimental to the well-being of society.

As well as concerning itself with questions of faith and Church reform, the Council busied itself vigorously with "secular" affairs: with the crusades; with the foundation of the Latin Empire in Constantinople; with the conflict over the successor in the dukedom of Toulouse, with the Magna Carta extorted from King John and with the conflict over Frederick II's accession as Emperor. The pope, as Christendom's ultimate authority, and his council, had to care not only for strictly ecclesiastical affairs but also with the worries and needs of the whole of Christendom and thus also for the Christian *imperium*. Pope Innocent III established the theory of the high-medieval apprehension of *Christianitas* most clearly in his *regestum super negotium Romani imperii*.[10] As Christ's representative, the pope, for him, is at once priest and king, and a royal priest and priestly king at that. The intrinsically spiritual power of the papacy is the basis of his priestly authority, from which his royal authority arises. Because invested with the *plenitudo potestatis ecclesiasticae* (the fullness of ecclesiastical authority), the pope stands above the body of the Church, the structure of which was viewed as a graded hierarchical pyramid. Just as the world's individual Churches are associated with the pope's *sacerdotium*, so the kingdoms of the Christian world are allied to the emperor who serves as Christendom's secular leader. Thus the emperor held precedence over all other Christian monarchs, but was not their lord and master. This hierarchical arrangement of the States has

---

[10]F. Kempf S.J., "Papsttum und Kaisertum bei Innozenz III," *Miscellanea historiae pontificiae* 19, Rome 1954; A Walz, OP, " 'Papst Kaiser' Innozenz III, Stimmen zur Deutung," in: *Sacerdozio e Regno da Gregorio VII a Bonifacio VIII*, Rome 1954, pp. 127-138.

nothing in common with the modern conception of sovereignty. It incorporated itself into Christendom, at the summit of which stood the pope.

The *sacerdotium* ranks above the *imperium*. Christendom's two supreme powers, papacy and empire, stand opposite one another like the sun and the moon. The emperor receives the glory of his position as Christendom's secular head from the pope much as the moon receives her light from the sun. The brilliance of his authority is in proportion to the extent of his co-operation with the pope; the further the emperor distances himself from the pope, the more he loses. Agreed, the *imperium* does not belong to the pope but it is his duty to look after it and to guide it in a state of emergency. This duty's origin lies in Pope Leo III's handing over of the empire (*translatio imperii*) to Charles the Great. It finds its full justification in the emperor's sacred coronation which remained the pope's exclusive right throughout the Middle Ages. The fully developed doctrine of the *translatio imperii* contains the following elements:

1. Charles the Great's coronation as emperor implied the handing over of the one Roman Empire from the East to the West, from Constantinople to Rome, though in practice, especially where negotiations over reunion were concerned, the existence of two emperors was upheld.

2. The handing over of imperial power took place in virtue of the authority of the Holy See.

3. The handing over was justified by the Church's need of a defence against two enemies.

4. By virtue of the *translatio imperii* the Holy See has the right to concern itself with questions concerning the *imperium*.

5. Should the protection of the Church require it the Holy See could effect a fresh *translatio imperii*.

These rights are supplemented by the right to crown the emperor, "for the emperor receives from the pope the ultimate imposition of hands vital to his actual elevation, in that he is blessed, crowned and invested with the empire by him".[11]

Thus it was that the peace between pope and emperor was strengthened by the Third Lateran Council (1179) and that Frederick II was confirmed as Emperor by the Fourth Lateran Council.

The Fourth Lateran Council was the most dazzling presentation of the medieval *Christianitas,* with its spiritual and secular aspects. Papal authority applied in the first instance to spiritual matters and it remained spiritual even when it was aimed indirectly at secular matters. The pope's and the council's legal title to deal with secular matters lay in the pope's pastoral supremacy, in his directive power over the entire Church which accords him supreme authority over the *populus Christianus.* As a sociological community Christendom was held together spiritually by the Christian faith and juridically by virtue of obedience to the pope. This *Christianitas* is the key to an understanding of the medieval, papal, general councils. The secular order and political authority were not absorbed by the spiritual order or ecclesiastical authority; they remained independent, each in its own domain. *Christianitas,* however, including as it did both the spiritual and the secular sphere, nevertheless demanded subordination in the spiritual domain only. In this respect the pope possessed a directive authority, peculiarly his own, over the emperor and the other secular powers and thus over all Christians. Christ's representative had become the crowning head of the whole of Christendom, of an organism vitalized by religious impulses, combining *imperium* and *sacerdotium* in one universal community. The pope combined these two powers, in fact independent of one another, in a spiritual dominion, which he directed through his spiritual authority, an authority that applied directly to spiritual matters

---

[11] "Innocent III, Deliberatio," in: *Regestum Innocentii III* 29, ed. F. Kempf, S.J., Rome 1947, p. 75.

and indirectly to the secular sphere as well. In this magnificent synthesis, brought to light by the Lateran Councils, the medieval world reached its zenith.

IV

The Councils of Lyons: the Freedom of the Church and Union with the Greeks

The emperors of the Hohenstaufen dynasty rebelled against the theocratic interpretation of the emperor's position as developed by Alexander III and Innocent III. Their conception of the imperial role was developed with the aid of the late Roman Justinian Constitutional law and Aristotelianism. Although they remained true to the idea of the all-embracing *Christianitas* and coronation by the pope, they stressed that imperial power was of a direct, divine origin. Cardinal Roland, the papal legate, had asked in Besançon (1175) from whom, if this was so, the emperor received his *imperium*, if not from the pope. To this Frederick Barbarossa made answer in his address to the German nations: "Kingship belongs to us by virtue of the election of the princes, and the *imperium* comes only from God", and the *imperium* is the empire "that has existed gloriously and undiminished since the foundation of Rome and the establishment of the Christian Church". Thus the conferment of the empire by the pope was rejected by simply ignoring the facts of Charles the Great's coronation by Leo III, as well as Otto the Great's by John XII. Cardinal Roland's question in Besançon was neither naïve nor presumptuous. It was a reference to the origin of the Western Empire. Pope Innocent III had said: "In view of its origin and its

24

aim the *imperium* belongs to the Apostolic Chair." The empire does not belong to the Holy See in such a way as to imply unhindered possession or feudal tenure that may be conferred at will. "Belongs to the Apostolic Chair" means that the pope has its welfare at heart and in an emergency his office will oblige him to intervene in its government. Innocent III laid stress on the ancient ecclesiastical right of the *translatio imperii* (transfer of the seat of empire) and fought against the new Staufer conception which diminished the pope's role in the origin and maintenance of the empire.[12] The Hohenstaufen and Guelph conflict over the throne, between Philip of Swabia and Otto IV of Brunswick gave the pope the opportunity to put into practice the rights to which he laid claim, namely that of examining the worthiness of a candidate (*Examinatio*—examination), the *approbatio*—approval of the candidate decreed worthy, the legal *confirmatio*—(confirmation) and the final *coronatio* (crowning). Frederick Barbarossa had explained in a letter to the German bishops that that man was emperor whom the Elector voted king, whom the Archbishop of Cologne consecrated king, and whom the pope anointed emperor.[13] Innocent III agreed that the German princes could elect whomsoever they pleased, but that it nevertheless remained the pope's exclusive right to determine whom he would crown emperor. He asserted this right when he intervened in the conflict over the throne and at first recognized Otto IV, whom he crowned emperor in 1209, only to have the Hohenstaufen Frederick II, who was under his guardianship, elected in

---

[12] F. Kempf, S.J., *Papsttum und Kaisertum, loc. cit.* pp. 95ff.
[13] *Ottonis et Rahewini gesta Friderici I imperatoris*, ed. G. Waitz, Hanover 1884, ch. 3, 17.   F. Kempf says that the medieval canonists narrowed down their enquiry to the *imperium* alone and had taken no account of the complicated structure of the Western Empire which had grown out of the German Kingdom and the Roman Empire, "blind as they were to the historical growth of forms", and so cut themselves off from the realities of the state.   F. Kempf, "Weltherrschaft des Papsttums?" in: *Stimmen der Zeit*, Vol. 158 (1955-56), p. 19.

Frankfurt and subsequently confirmed as emperor through the Fourth Lateran Council in 1212.

In the background of the ensuing struggle between Frederick II and the popes Gregory IX and Innocent IV stood the antithesis between the Hohenstaufen and the papal conception of the empire. This antithesis became under Innocent IV a fight over the Church's liberty.

Innocent IV had developed yet further the theocratic viewpoint of his predecessors: the pope's indivisible fullness of power included fullness of power in the spiritual sphere as well as in the temporal sphere. Because Innocent no longer believed he could settle through negotiations the conflict (begun during the pontificate of his predecessor, Gregory IX) with the emperor over the respective rights of Church and empire, he convoked a general council at Lyons on 3rd January, 1245. Innocent IV put forward Frederick II's persecution of the Church as the Council's main concern. On 17th July, 1245, the Council pronounced a sentence of deposition against Frederick, who, they said, was a perjurer, a disturber of the peace, and suspect of heresy.[14]

The Council also dealt with Christendom's other problems, of which the pope had spoken in his inaugural discourse: a crusade to reconquer Jerusalem, the repulse of future Mongol

---

[14]M. B. Carra de Vaux Saint Cyr, O.P., adds: Il n'alla pas d'ailleurs sans récrimination: le condamné et d'autres princes avec lui se prirent à nier le droit du Pape à déposer les souverains. La mort de Frédéric II, la victoire, en apparence si complète, qui s'ensuivit pour l'Eglise, peuvent bien couvrir pour un temps ces rumeurs: bientôt nous verrons jusqu'ou iront ces lézardes dans l'imposant édifice théocratique du Moyen âge chrétien (in *Lumière et Vie*, *loc. cit.*, p. 27).—While Frederick II, in his puffed up delight in absolute imperial power, which was tending towards the constitutional law of Justinian, contradicts both by his measures against freedom of the Church and the Council and by many aspects of his moral conduct the ideal of the Christian ruler, the French King Louis IX, the Saint, realised it by never using his power for his own ends but always in the service of good. He endeavoured to avoid exacerbating the struggle between pope and emperor, discouraged the deposition of Frederick II and even accorded him later the full imperial title, cf. also C. A. Willemsen, "Friedrich II", in: *LThK*, Vol. 4 (1960), pp. 380-381.

irruptions, the reorganization of the Church's legislation with regard to judicial procedure, and the pressure on the Latin empire of Constantinople.

It had not escaped Innocent IV that it was dangerous to connect the reunion of the Eastern Churches with the afore-mentioned Latin empire. He negotiated successfully with the Greek Emperor John III over a union and gave notice of a general council to meet in Constantinople, which, however, came to nothing because both the pope and the Greek emperor died before the project could develop.

The negotiations for union were resumed later, when Michael Palaeologus had driven the Latins from Constantinople and had had himself crowned *Basileus*. The second Council of Lyons saw the completion of the union of the Greek Church with the Church of Rome. The Greek deputies agreed to the prescribed profession of faith, which meant the recognition of papal primacy, the septenary number of the sacraments and the doctrine of purgatory. Once the Greeks, by participating in the singing of the Roman Catholic Creed, had confessed their faith in the *filioque* clause, they were permitted to retain the traditional text of their Creed. For various reasons the union was short-lived : the emperor had supported it only from political motives; points in which the respective theologies were at loggerheads were not discussed with the Greeks during the Councils and the union encountered bitter and deep-seated resistance among many bishops and even more so among the monastic orders and the laity. When Pope Martin IV (1281-5) gave his support to the King of Naples' plans of conquest in the East the union collapsed completely.

The second Council of Lyons was also a gathering of *Christianitas,* to which not only bishops were invited, but also abbots, cathedral chapters, representatives of the orders of knights, Christian kings and princes and the Greek emperor. Apart from union with the Greeks, a new crusade and Church reform were among themes discussed. The decree *Ubi periculum,* on papal elections, which for the most part is still in force today, was accepted by the council. "The second Council of Lyons was like the fourth Lateran in its ecumenical representation as an assembly of the whole of Christendom. It resembled the latter too in being a platform on which political decisions were taken. The quarrel between Alfonso of Castile and Rudolf von Hapsburg for the imperial crown was decided by the Pope accepting the engagements undertaken by Rudolf and urging his rival to forego his claims. The formal recognition of Rudolf followed the conclusion of the Council on 26th September 1274. That put an end to the unfortunate interregnum. James I of Aragon, who had appeared at the Council in order to get the Pope to crown him, left in dudgeon because the Pope demanded of him homage and tribute in money. The king of France gave up the princedom of Venaissin, which had long been the property of the Pope, but had up to then been administered by a vassal. A deputation from the Great Khan of Mongolia sought an alliance against Egypt. It did not obtain one, but a member of the deputation accepted baptism."[15]

V

The Council of Vienne in the Shadow of Boniface VIII

Pope Boniface VIII vigorously maintained his theocratic position in the structure of the *Christianitas.* He embodied the *sacerdotium's* strongest claims against the *imperium* and his demands remain problematic even if charitably interpreted.[16]

---

[15]H. Jedin, *Ecumenical Councils in the Catholic Church, loc. cit.*
[16]F. Kempf, S.J., *Papsttum und Kaisertum, loc. cit.,* p. 300.

His doctrine of the two swords in the pope's hands, the one spiritual, the other temporal, though not new was decidedly characteristic of that particular period. His attitude to the Church's role in her relations with the secular domain was conditioned by the prevailing circumstances. On this subject Pope Pius XII expressed himself very clearly in an address to the tenth Congress of Historians delivered in Rome on 7th September, 1955: "This medieval conception was conditioned by its era. Those acquainted with the sources will surely admit that there would have been yet more cause for amazement if this conception had never arisen."[17]

Just as Boniface VIII before his abduction by the emissaries of Philip the Fair, King of France, the prelude to the "exile of Avignon", had strictly defined papal supremacy over Christendom's spiritual and temporal spheres, so, similarly, Emperor Henry VII pulled no punches in his proclamation, prior to the collapse of the imperial power, of his own conception of "empire". In a circular letter dated 1312 about the imperial coronation Henry gave his readers to understand that God had ordained that "all men, grouped in their various empires and countries, are subject to but one ruler, so that the world's structure can develop yet more gloriously".[18] This interpretation of the situation is in accordance with Dante's "World Monarchy", the territory of which is the whole of the inhabited world, and the Roman Emperor, to whom all peoples and nations owe allegiance, is its sole ruler. The German Electors decide, by virtue of their divine mandate, upon the *curator orbis,* whom the pope then crowns emperor. This was a glorification of the

---

[17] *AAS*, Vol. 47 (1955), p. 678. Cf. also the explanation of the temporary factors conditioning certain medieval ideas of law (the right of deposition), published by Pope Pius IX in July, 1871. This text, which first appeared in Civiltà Cattolica, 1871, p. 485, can be found in C. Butler, *The Vatican Council.* This complicated issue is thoroughly dealt with by F. Kempf, "Caput Christianitatis", in: *Stimmen der Zeit*, Vol. 158 (1955-56), pp. 91-100.

[18] *MGH Const.* IV, 2, 802. Henry VII's mother tongue was French. He felt himself to be a universal emperor—not as just a national emperor but as the Roman Emperor.

emperor conception which had long been contradicted by the reality which the then developing national states presented.

While Emperor Henry VII was on his way to Rome where Dante hailed him as universal emperor, the last of the general councils of the central period of the Middle Ages met in Vienne (1311), "at the crossroads of two worlds". Once again Christendom's bishops gathered round the pope to discuss its affairs. For the first time "procurators" appeared, as representatives of those bishops unable to attend in person. The Council is famous for the suppression of the Order of the Templars brought about by overwhelming pressure brought to bear by Philip the Fair, King of France. This was symptomatic of a period of weakness which the papacy was experiencing and which is linked with a collapse of medieval *Universalism*. National States, as we know them today, originated at this time, and France became the first great European power with a centralised administration. The constitutional characteristic of these states was their sovereignty, their political independence and consequent dislike of outside interference. Theirs now was the power to mould their own community life in their own territory.

VI

The ecclesiology of the General Councils of the Central Period of the Middle Ages

"The papal general councils of the second half of the Middle Ages had been the work of the reform Papacy. All of them had been convoked and presided over by the popes. Like the early councils they were bishops' councils but enlarged by the participation of abbots, representatives of cathedral chapters and even of secular power. Though the latter were not entitled to a vote (strictly speaking) they had the right of making themselves heard in matters that concerned them. The pope gave their final form to the conciliar decrees and embodied a large number of them in the papal code of laws. At the councils he appears as the apex of a pyramid which included both the Church and the community of all Christian peoples."[19]

The following points are worth noting :

1. The pope's primacy, theologically established by Leo the Great and emphasized by him at the Council of Chalcedon, had fully developed. The pope alone convoked the council and he it was who decided who should take part.[20] He decided upon the agenda and personally led the discussions, and it was his consent that made the decrees valid. "The Pope felt justified in editing the decisions taken at the council, in revising them where necessary and finally enforcing them".[21] A characteristic of an ecumenical council is the participation and consent of the pope. Four years before the first Lateran council a synod met in Rheims which resembled the Lateran Council in its reform decrees and in the number of its participators. In spite of this the Rheims' synod was not ecumenical, which the Lateran Councils were, as the pope convoked them as general synods and awarded them general application.[22]

2. The papal general councils of the central period of the Middle Ages demonstrate a very real degree of co-operation between pope, bishops and other participators. Heiler's contentions that the bishops were degraded to the role of "tools of

---

[19]H. Jedin, *loc. cit.*
[20]The fact that Philip had any influence on the list of the bishops to be summoned to the Council of Vienne was unusual and an indication of Clement V's weakness.
[21]H. Jedin, *loc. cit.*, with reference to Clement V.
[22]It would be desirable to have a historical, theological, canonical and sociological study of the papacy from the viewpoint of the general councils of the Middle Ages.

an almighty pope" is quite unfounded. There was freedom of speech and also a right to disagree with any suggestions tendered. In fact, the reason for the good effect of the reform legislation was precisely because it had been discussed by pope and bishops collectively.[23]

3. In order to understand the full significance of the participation in these councils not only of abbots and cathedral chapters but also of emperors, kings and princes, and the discussion, in a synod, of political, social and economic matters, it must be remembered that the councils of the central period of the Middle Ages were Christendom's rallying points. *Christianitas* was a community that included *sacerdotium* and *imperium*, with pope and emperor as spiritual and temporal heads; but the former ranked higher. All emperors recognized the pope's historic role in the foundation of the Western Empire in 800, and they all, up to Charles V (1530), received their imperial crown at the pope's hands, and hand in hand with acceptance of the crown went their own particular position vis-à-vis other crowned western monarchs, and also a spiritual relationship to the Church whose protector and defender they were. There was no emperor who had denied this, not even Frederick II, who, as Martin Grabmann has pointed out, was neither a pagan nor a freethinker in the modern sense, but one who remained inside the framework of the medieval *Weltanschauung*.[24] The councils of the central period of the Middle Ages presupposed in their political and social measures the existence of only one Church and one Christian Empire, which together constituted Christendom. Inside this structure the pope, as *caput spirituale* (spiritual head), made terms with the emperor, as *caput temporale* (temporal head). The papal general councils confirmed the Concordat of Worms bet-

---

[23]H. Jedin, *loc. cit.*
[24]M. Grabmann, "Kaiser Friedrich II und sein Verhältnis zur aristotelischen Philosophie", in: *Mittelalterliches Geistesleben* Vol. II, (1936), pp. 136-137.

ween Calixtus II and Henry V as well as the Peace of Venice between Alexander III and Frederick Barbarossa. They concerned themselves with the business of confirming an emperor on his throne and of deposing him, and they regulated the affairs of Christian kingdoms. There is, then, no place here for the modern conception of Church-State relationships, that is, an automatic assumption that the two are autonomous communities, for the particular form of these councils arises out of their historical setting and can only be understood if the medieval conception of *Christianitas* is understood.

In a very thorough analysis of these matters, Friedrich Kempf has shown that the medieval Church, the popes and their councils, in fact never worked for universal, political dominion; it was rather their intention to preserve the autonomy of the ecclesiastical and civil authorities. The concept of "Christendom" was not one whose purpose was to guarantee the pope political or civil power, but one that envisaged a leadership inside the Christian world and emanating from spiritual authority.[25]

"To comprehend exactly what is meant by *Christianitas* is not easy. It means the community of all Christians, not so much in the ecclesiastical as in a socio-political sense, a type of fatherland, almost a *supra*national nation; a collection of Christian peoples and nations rather than one single state—an organism the essence of which is at once juridical and spiritual. A common faith and membership of the same Church held the whole together—a whole vitalized by the Church. Because the pope presided over the Church, he was also the head of *Christianitas*—but only by virtue of his ecclesiastical power; peoples and nations kept their own identity, independent of the Church, and their own political and cultural duties."[26]

[25]F. Kempf, S.J., "Weltherrschaft des mittelalterlichen Papsttums?", in: *Stimmen der Zeit*, Vol. 158 (1955-56), pp. 13-23.
[26]F. Kempf, S.J., "Caput Christianitatis," in: *Stimmen der Zeit*, Vol. 158 (1955-56), p. 94; cf. *ibid.* pp. 98-99.

The notion of *Christianitas* represented the attempt to differentiate the Christian world from the Church and yet, even so, to link it with the Church. As it happened, so far-reaching was the communion between the two, that the Church exceeded her own domain and affected Christendom's temporal domain. The Christendom confronting the Church was not a clearly defined, legally regulated institution; for this a central power endowed with definite legal supremacy was lacking. The emperor's authority sprang merely from the sacred nature of his imperial dignity and from his duty to protect the Church. Christendom was never a national political organization, and the kings of France and England refused to concede to the emperor a constitutional position superior to their own.

In this Christendom *sacerdotium* and *imperium,* spiritual and temporal, faith and knowledge, mystery and perception, community and individual, were bound up in one all-embracing unity, and even in the event of a clash of these inherent forces, this was only over questions relating to the interpretation and application of the established order, which was not in principle disputed by the parties involved. Philosophers and poets, such as Thomas Aquinas and Dante, strove after an ever deeper understanding, an ever closer description of this divinely-willed Christian order.[27] The scope allowed to individual creativeness is witnessed by the undeniable richness of medieval culture.

Yet there may already, as in Latin Averroism, be discerned some cracks in the impressive fabric of Christendom which led to its collapse in the late Middle Ages. Marsiglio of Padua's treatise *Defensor pacis,* written at the instigation of the emperor Lewis of Bavaria, had a significant part to play in this collapse. The work purports to give the theoretic basis of the

---

[27] Cf. J. Spörl, "Otto von Freising", in: *Stimmen der Zeit,* Vol. 163, (1958-59), pp. 145 ff.

imperial authority, maintaining that the empire rests on the sovereign will of the world-wide Roman nation.

Marsiglio likewise makes the legitimacy of the ecclesiastical hierarchy depend on the will of the Christian peoples who are represented at the highest level by councils made up of clerics and elected laymen. This view strikes at the ecclesiological foundations of all church dignities. It finds historical parallels in the summoning of the Colonna cardinals to a general council to oppose Boniface VIII, and in the appeal by the Sachsen-hausens to Lewis of Bavaria to attend a general council to oppose the excommunication with which John XXII was threatening him in 1324.

CHAPTER THREE

The Councils of the Late Middle Ages and their Ecclesiological Importance

WHEN the Council of Vienne met, "ideas were already being aired which ascribed to the general councils a far more extensive role than any they had hitherto fulfilled. There was question of nothing less than that the council, as the final and supreme authority, should restore the unity of the Church in spite of the divided Papacy, and carry out an urgently needed reform of the Church, both in her head and in her members (*reformatio in capite et membris*).

The great Eastern schism gave these ideas a yet stronger impulse, though many years were to pass before any attempt was made to put them into effect. The Great Schism was not a result of the trouble between pope and emperor. The relationship between *sacerdotium* and *imperium* which had caused the medieval councils so much concern had by now faded into the background behind the fresh problem of the council's relationship to the pope, which the split in Church Unity had pushed to the fore. The emperor's position as guardian of the universal Church, and as the world's consecrated political leader, was, through the schism, once again brought home to Christendom, which, by this time, had lost its medieval compactness. For this reason Emperor Sigismund had an

---

[1]H. Jedin, *loc. cit.*

36

important role to play, not only in the council's convocation but also in seeing it through once it had begun. On 30th October, 1413, he announced, in a proclamation addressed to the whole of Christendom, the General Council of Constance, to which Pope John reluctantly agreed. Finally, on 9th December, 1413, he himself convoked the council.

The three late-medieval councils of Constance, Basle, Ferrara-Florence and the fifth Lateran Council are known for their handling of such problems as the Eastern Schism, heated discussions on conciliar theory, reunion of the Eastern Churches, and ecclesiastical reform. The fifth Lateran Council conformed to the tradition of the papal general councils of the central period of the Middle Ages. It condemned "Conciliarism", and refused to acknowledge the idea of a parliamentary "representation", as proposed at Constance and Basle.

I

The Council of Constance and the endangering of ecclesiology by Conciliarism

This council, which lasted from 1414-1418, terminated the Great Schism, elected Martin V pope, condemned John Hus, and drew up concordats with five nations. It published the decree *Sacrosancta* on the superiority of the council over the pope as well as the decree *Frequens* on the periodic convocation of councils. Pope Martin V condemned the conciliar theory expressed in the decree *Sacrosancta* by forbidding appeal from the pope to the council.

In accordance with the decree *Frequens*, which stipulated that a council should be convoked every five years, Pope Martin issued invitations for a council at Pavia, which he subsequently changed to Siena, only to find that even Siena had to be abandoned owing to poor attendance. After a further period of seven years a council was convoked at Basle, which, under Pope Eugene IV, lasted from 1431-7, attempted to put the conciliar theory into practice and to constitute itself the Church's supreme judicial and administrative authority. The council's order of procedure was comparable with that of a modern parliament. When votes were counted, the bishops accounted for no more than a tenth of all those entitled to vote.

Pope Eugene IV, who in 1435 and 1436, had already protested against a number of conciliar decisions, broke with those at Basle in the summer of 1437, and on 18th September, 1437, transferred the council to Ferrara. Here he had already won the support of the Greeks against the majority at the Council of Basle. The Greeks wanted to open negotiations concerning the restoration of Church unity.

Conciliarism, as demonstrated both in theory and in practice at the councils of Constance and Basle, now contradicted the Church's God-given structure. Pierre d'Ailly, Cardinal of Cambrai, demanded a right to vote, not only for bishops and abbots, but also for doctors of theology and canon law, and for Christian princes and their ambassadors. According to d'Ailly, the fact that formerly only bishops had had the conclusive right to vote was by virtue of their special selection for that purpose on grounds of proved sanctity and great learning. This opinion received a majority approval. Indeed, they went still further by admitting at Constance a national vote.

The ideas of conciliar theorists such as d'Ailly, Gerson, Dietrich von Nieheim and Zabarella, are traceable not only to Marsiglio of Padua's idea of sovereignty of the people in *Defensor pacis*, or to William of Ockham's similar ideas in the

Dialogus, but are in fact rooted further back in the legal view of the medieval guilds. This notion understood the Church as a corporation in which authority resides in its members and is therefore theirs to wield. In a medieval guild all members take part in decisions which concern their well-being as a whole. The extent to which the members may use this authority is in direct ratio to the importance of the decisions to the members as a whole. Applied to the Church, this theory (already carried out by John of Paris, d.1306) meant that authority resided not only with the pope as head of the Church but also with the members. But the members transfer their right to the pope by virtue of his election by the cardinals; it is, however, "open to them to rescind this transfer should the pope err in a matter of faith or abuse his power to the detriment of the Church".[2]

These ideas constituted a retreat from the traditional conciliar attitude and were a complete contradiction of the Church's hierarchical structure, in which authority comes from above and not from below; from Jesus Christ through the Holy Spirit who guides the Vicar of Christ; but not from the members of the Mystical Body.

Hubert Jedin has shown how the later attitude of the reformers towards both Church and Council is connected with late-medieval conciliarism and, of course, how much further it went.[3]

---

[2] H. Jedin, *loc. cit.*
[3] H. Jedin, *Geschichte des Konzils von Trient,* Vol. I, Freiburg in Breisgau, 1949, pp. 1-132.

II

The Council of Basle-Ferrara-Florence and Union
with the Greeks

Pope Eugene IV had suggested Constantinople as a suitable
meeting-place. But opposition from Basle thwarted the plan.
Finally other suggestions materialized: the pope proposed
Italy, and those at Basle suggested participation in their own
assembly either in Basle or in Lyons. The Byzantine Emperor,
John VIII, presented with a choice, opted for the pope's
suggestion, because the Greeks had always regarded the pope
as the only person to deal with when union was at stake.
Strengthened by the Emperor's support, the pope, on 18th
September, 1437, transferred the Council of Basle to Ferrara
and on 9th April, 1438, inaugurated the council of union with
the Greeks. This he did in the presence of more than seventy
western bishops, the Byzantine Emperor, Patriarch Joseph of
Constantinople, Archbishops Markos Eugenikos of Ephesus.
Bessarion of Nicea and Isidore of Kiev, as well as representatives of the patriarchs of Alexandria, Antioch and Jerusalem.
There were also other Eastern bishops, priests and theologians,
the number of whom increased as time went on.[4]

After Easter began the discussions on controversial questions,
which resolved themselves under four main headings:

1. Teaching on the procession of the Holy Spirit; Rome
taught and maintained that the Holy Spirit proceeded from the

---

[4]Cf. the outstanding work of Joseph Gill, S.J., *The Council of Florence*,
Cambridge, 1959.

Father and from the Son—*tamquam ab uno principio et unica spiratione* (as though from one principle and one spiration). The discussion on the doctrine led first of all, in October, 1438, at the request of the Greeks, to the question of whether the addition to the Credo by the Roman Church of the *Filioque* was permissible. This time-consuming controversy took up all of fourteen sessions. When the Romans explained that they viewed the *Filioque* as an explanation of *ex Patre procedit* and not as an addition (just as former councils had explained the *depositum* of the bible), the Greeks were presented with something quite new.

The emperor himself took an active part in the discussions, defended his bishops' viewpoint, influenced the spirit of their participation and urged them to persevere in spite of their boredom with the council. He was concerned as guardian of the Eastern Church not to concede any of its traditions, and at the same time to do all in his power to reach an understanding with the Roman Church and thus to save the rest of his Christian empire. The Greek bishops were similarly minded, yet not for one moment were they prepared, for political reasons, to depart from tradition, to which they felt themselves in conscience bound. Both Greeks and Romans dealt with the union question in sincere accordance with their beliefs. The impassioned debates, which almost caused the council's downfall, bear witness to the freedom of discussion and decision which prevailed there.

After the transfer of the council to Florence on 16th January, 1439, eight public sessions with both sides present were devoted to discussing the dogma of the procession of the Holy Ghost and to smoothing out the path to a settlement of the controversy. Pope Eugene IV did not let the difficulties discourage him. He and his prelates made valiant attempts to bring about an agreement based on Holy Scripture and tradition. He was well able to adapt himself to the circumstances and agreed to

41

forego public sessions to begin with and have the issues debated in private among the theologians, with Greeks and Romans separated but keeping one another informed. This method proved successful and set the way open. Bessarion and the Greek lay-theologian George Scholarios strove successfully to demonstrate the harmony of eastern and western tradition about the procession of the Holy Ghost. On 8th June, 1439, the Greeks accepted the article about the procession of the Holy Ghost from the Father and the Son, in which the Greek formula of procession from the Father through the Son (*ex patre per filium procedere spiritum sanctum*) was acknowledged and made clearer.[5]

2. The use of unleavened bread in the Eucharist. It is hard for us today to understand how this could provide such a serious controversy. But for the symbolically minded early Church it was a question of vital theological importance. The Latins used unleavened bread to symbolize the purity and holiness of Our Lord's body born of the Virgin Mary (cf. 1 Cor. 5 : 7-8). The Greeks used leavened bread to symbolize the pure and perfect humanity of Our Lord in the sense of the Council of Chalcedon, for unleavened bread seemed lifeless and incomplete to their way of thinking. Closely connected with this question in the Council's proceedings was that of the form of the Eucharist and significance of the Epiclesis. There was final agreement about the validity of consecration with the use of either bread in accordance with the respective custom of East and West.[6] On 5th July, 1439, Bessarion announced on behalf

---

[5] *Decretum pro Graecis*, Denz 691.

[6] *Ibid.* Denz. 692. There was even agreement over the question of the Epiclesis. The Epiclesis is an invocation of the Holy Ghost to "show" or "make" the bread as Our Lord's body and the wine as His blood an effective means of salvation for those partaking. Since this invocation is to be found after the account of the institution in almost all Eastern liturgies and has a similar form to the words of consecration, there was a controversy over the Epiclesis going back to the 14th century. This controversy suffered from a lack of knowledge of liturgical history on both sides. J. P. de Jong states that even the so-called

of the Greeks their recognition that transubstantiation took place at the uttering of Christ's words of institution, as Chrysostom in particular had taught.

3. The doctrine of purgatory. The fathers of the Council had first dealt with this matter at Ferrara. There was agreement about a state of purification and the effectiveness of intercession for the departed souls in their suffering, without going into further details as to the nature of this suffering.[7] A wise limitation!

4. The primacy of the Bishop of Rome. This controversial doctrine provided the most difficulties and gave rise to heated disputes. John of Ragusa opened the discussion by bringing forward evidence from tradition in favour of the primacy and making the pope's primacy of jurisdiction stand out strongly over the claims of the Eastern patriarch. The Greeks, in fact, were prepared to recognize the Bishop of Rome's primacy, but with two reservations

(a) a council could not be ecumenical unless the East Roman Emperor and the Eastern Patriarchs took part;

(b) it was not permissible for the Patriarchs to appeal to the Pope. The Pope was not allowed to hear these appeals, nor the Patriarchs to plead before his tribunal. The most he could do would be to send arbitrators to the respective ecclesiastical province with powers to settle the controversy in the presence of both parties.

As Pope Eugene IV did not recognize these reservations the conference threatened to fall through. Those who supported reunion spoke with both the Pope and the Emperor and

---

consecration-epiclesis is really a communion epiclesis "which gives symbolical expression to what happens at the words of Consecration". Cf. J. P. de Jong, "Epiklese", in *LThK*, Vol. III, 2nd. impr. Cols. 935-937. In Florence the Greeks stressed, mainly because of the pronouncements of St John Chrysostom, that they ascribed an effect of consecration to the words of institution.

[7]*Decretum pro Graecis*, Denz. 693.

managed to obtain a further discussion between delegates from both sides. In this small working group Latins and Greeks finally found a formula to which both sides agreed : the Pope was recognized as the Supreme Pastor and Teacher of all Christendom "without any detraction from the privileges and rights of the Eastern Patriarch". This formula was couched in the widest possible terms and was the last concession the Latin supporters of reunion were allowed to make and the Greek bishops were prepared to agree to. Pope Eugene accepted it, thereby removing the last doctrinal difficulty. The resolutions were worded by both sides and formulated in a decree whose text was drawn up on 5th July, 1439, and on the same evening signed by the participators, 115 from the West and 33 from the East, the Greek signatures being headed by that of the East Roman Emperor. The only abstentions were Markos Eugenikos of Ephesus and the Bishop of Stauropolis. The latter, however, added his signature later.

On 6th July, 1439, the Pope celebrated Mass in Florence cathedral before the assembled Latins and Greeks. The Bull of Reunion—*Laetentur Caeli*—was read out in Latin and Greek during the ceremony and was assented to by the Fathers of the Council. The Greek text was recognized by the East Roman Emperor, twenty Greek prelates, six clerics and six representatives of Greek monasteries. The union of the Greek Orthodox Church with Rome was complete.[8]

Of equal, if not greater, importance to our present situation is the lesson in method to be learned from the theological work done at the Florence Council. It required a very special form of theological work to overcome the deadlocks, which seemed hopeless at the outset, and bring about reunion. The Latins tried at first with a dazzling display of scholastic argument and

---

[8]Cf. B. Schultze, S.J., "Das Letzte Ökumenische Einigungskonzil theologisch gesehen", in: *Orientalia Christiana Periodica*, Vol. XXV (1959), pp. 288-309.

thought they would be able to convince the Greeks by sheer force of logic. It is worthy of note that this method made no impression on the Orthodox but rather repelled and embittered them. Metropolitan Isidore of Kiev, a firm supporter of union with Rome, described the delight of the Latins in syllogisms and conclusions as a mania and added: "I am sorry to say that the Latins have by this means made the rift wider and the discord greater and more bitter". Agreement was attained by a completely different approach and by other methods. No way to reunion was found until Greeks and Latins patiently rediscovered the tradition they had held in common for a thousand years and both sides realized there was no reason to set its own way of looking at the questions against the other; until they recognized the unity of their faith deep down in this common tradition and were ready to respect the theological characteristics of the other. A classic example of this was given by the *Filioque* discussions. Patriarch Joseph of Constantinople declared on 3rd June, 1439, that the Greeks had been led entirely by the authority of their Fathers concerning the procession of the Holy Ghost.

A further lesson from these discussions is the extraordinary importance of non-theological factors in coming to an agreement. We are human beings wanting to make contact again with one another, and even if we strive after this in a Christian spirit we are not pure spirits, and the human aspects of our encounter are extremely important psychologically. These imponderables played a very large part at the Council of Florence. Both sides had to learn to accustom themselves to the different cast of mind of their opposite number, and seriously consider their claims, even, for instance, in matters of protocol.

And it was the non-theological factors which in a few years' time were to wreck the union. There was on both sides a lack of spiritual preparation for lasting union. Latins and Greeks alike made serious psychological blunders. Even during the

Council, Bishop Markos of Ephesus was openly opposed to reunion, and alone among the assembled Greeks refused to sign the Union decree. It was wrong of the Latins to look upon him for this as a black sheep and to treat him unkindly and unfairly. Furthermore Pope Eugene IV did not sufficiently appreciate the influence of George Scholarios, who throughout the council supported reunion, with the result that this theologian felt himself slighted by the Pope. It was this perhaps which prepared for George Scholarios' changed attitude when as Patriarch of Constantinople he later became the soul of resistance to union with the Roman Catholic Church. On the other side the East Roman Emperor John VIII Palaeologus was remarkably uncommitted throughout the Council, but on his return to Constantinople remained too long inactive against the propaganda of the opponents of reunion. His task was not easy. He had some influence on his bishops but scarcely any on the monks who were the leaders of public opinion where reunion was concerned. How was the Emperor to overcome the passions and resentments inflamed by the crusades? Western aid to the threatened capital proved inadequate, and in November 1444 the crusaders sent to the relief of Constantinople were defeated at Varna on the Black Sea. John saw himself on his own against this great danger to the Empire and his call for help was in vain. His successor, Constantine XI, was a determined supporter of union, but his death at the defeat of Constantinople by the Turks on 29th May, 1453 ended the union. It also ended the East Roman Empire which had been for so long the bulwark, even for Western Christendom, against the advance of Mohammedanism. The new rulers of Constantinople saw to it that the rift in the Church remained open.

The lesson for us from all this can only be to prepare carefully for any rapprochement, not to rush matters or use dialectic means of persuasion, and to keep away from any form of

pressure or undesirable influence. Pope John XXIII, in his
letter to the clergy of Venice on 23rd April, 1959, emphasized
that Catholics and Orthodox must first meet as brothers, and
grow closer and more accustomed to one another, before there
can be any thought of reunion. Humility, patience and charity
must be the mark of all discussions between separated brothers
about the unity of faith.

III

The Fifth Lateran Council

Louis XII of France used conciliar theories as a political
weapon in his war with Pope Julius II. At his instigation some
schismatic Cardinals called a *Conciliabulum* at Pisa in 1511
which renewed the decrees of Constance, transferred to Milan
in 1512 and came to an inglorious end at Lyons after Louis
had let it drop. The *Conciliabulum* of Pisa was the cause of the
fifth Lateran Council being convoked by Julius II on 19th April,
1512. "The last Lateran Council, the eighteenth of the general
councils, was intended to follow on from the papal councils
of the central period of the Middle Ages and thereby stood
apart from the two councils of the previous century. Super-
vised and presided over by the Pope in Rome, it was almost
exclusively composed of Italian bishops. At the opening
session on 10th May, 1512, there were fifteen cardinals and
seventy-nine bishops. The Pope decided its agenda and
appointed the officials. The decrees took the form of papal
bulls".[9]

After the death of Julius II on 21st February, 1513, his
successor Leo X went on with the Lateran Council. He signed

[9] H. Jedin, *loc. cit.*

47

a concordat with Francis I of France and had it confirmed by the council on 19th December, emphasizing that this confirmation merely gave additional solemnity to an already valid treaty.

The Constitution *Pastor aeternus* expressly condemned the "Pragmatic Sanction", which had been published in 1438 and was strongly influenced by conciliaristic ideas, and clearly taught the supremacy of the Pope over the General Council. The Pope's teaching office had overcome conciliarism, and in this respect the Fifth Lateran Council marks the victory of traditional doctrine about the constitution of the Church over the destructive tendencies of Constance and Basle which struck at the whole basis of ecclesiology.

The council was not so successful in carrying out the long awaited reform of the Church. Giles of Viterbo, the General of the Augustinians, had made clear in his sermon at the opening of the Council the leading motive of all attempts at Catholic reform when he said : "Men must be transformed by what is holy, not what is holy by men". The Camaldolese, Giustiniani and Quirini, had offered suggestions for reform to Leo X which concerned not only a revision and adaptation of Church Law for the needs of changed circumstances and a putting in order of religious life and the liturgy, but also new discussions for reunion with the Eastern Church and even the question of missionary work in the recently discovered New World.[10]

Only a few of these suggestions were dealt with by the council and its achievements were even fewer. A great opportunity of warding off impending dangers through renovation and reform was missed. On 16th March, 1517, Martin Luther nailed his ninety-five theses to the church door at Wittenberg. Three years later the spark had become a raging fire and the

---

[10]*ibid.*

cry for a new council rang throughout the land. When at last the Council of Trent opened on 13th December, 1545, the crack was on the point of becoming a great rift. Would the Council be able to seal this crack and restore the unity of the Church?

CHAPTER FOUR

The Two Councils of Modern Times and the Development of the Doctrine of the Church

THE Council of Trent and Vatican Council, just as much as the earlier councils, were gatherings of the Catholic Church, represented by its bishops assembling in union with the Pope. But at the same time these councils were no longer, like those of the central period of the Middle Ages, gatherings of a universal Christendom united in one faith. The word "Christendom" did, it is true, feature prominently in Pope Paul III's bull of 22nd May, 1542, convoking the Council : the Council was to work for "the welfare of Christendom" and the Pope hoped, through it, "to restore peace and church unity to the Christian people", while admitting sorrowfully that the unity of Christendom had been "almost completely torn apart by dissensions, quarrels and heresies".

In the same Bull of Convocation the Pope spoke at length about the role of the Emperor and the King of France, whose support he considered essential for the unhindered proceedings of the Council. Because of this, said Paul III, he had wished to hold this general council only with the full agreement of the Christian princes, until the continuously deteriorating state of Christendom forced him to delay no longer and to announce the convocation. But once again the Council did not take place because the war between Francis I and the Emperor broke out afresh two weeks later. As a result Pope and Emperor agreed at Busseto to a postponement of the Council. It was not until the Peace of Crépy, at which Francis I declared himself agreeable to the opening of the Council and promised the participation of the French bishops, that the obstacles were removed, and the Council was finally convened on 15th March 1545 at Trent.

In this Bull an invitation was extended not only to patriarchs, archbishops, bishops and abbots but also to the Emperor and the most Christian King of France, as well as to dukes and princes. They were to send representatives if they were prevented from coming in person. The aims of the Council, apart from the preservation of the truths of faith in their entirety and the reform of morals, were expressly stated to be "the unity and harmony of Christian people and princes and defence against the onslaughts of heathens and unbelievers who threaten to overwhelm the whole of Christendom."

It can be seen that Trent forms a bridge between the councils of the High Middle Ages and the Vatican Council. Yet its particular form more closely resembles the Vatican Council than the Fourth Lateran Council, since at the time of Trent "Christendom" was no longer a politically represented unity, and powerful national states had emerged which decisively rejected the Emperor's claim to take the lead in questions concerning Christendom as a whole, or else made this claim for themselves. The Bull of Convocation named "the Most Christian King of France", along with Emperor Charles V—"the Roman Emperor, in all ages the Augmentor of the Empire"—as "the two mightiest supports and powers of Christendom." And so this Christendom is, in spite of all, still a reality and remains so in the centuries to come. Even if its universal representation has been weakened by differences of belief and modern nationalism, it still stays rooted in the minds of Western peoples. The states being formed were indeed secular in that their jurisdiction was exercised in the secular rather than in the spiritual realm, but they were by no means *secularized* in the sense of the ideas stemming from the French Revolution. There was as yet no separation of Church and State; on the contrary, the Church had to protect itself from becoming a new sort of State Church, such as absolutist rulers were aiming at or had actually succeeded in bringing about.

To defend its unity and freedom the post-medieval Church has held its councils as purely ecclesiastical assemblies of bishops under the direction of the Pope. As episcopal councils, without any secular representatives, they are like the councils of the early Church; with regard to the clearly defined pre-eminence of the Pope they resemble those of the High Middle Ages. The Tridentine and Vatican Councils have given the Church its present form, assured its unity and opened up new possibilities for the furtherance of its catholicity.

I

The Council of Trent

Recent investigations into ecclesiastical history have produced evidence that the question of councils was at the time of the Reformation very much to the fore in discussions about church politics and theology. But behind the demand for a "free general council of Christians on German soil" lay a new concept of the Church, its sacramental basis and its hierarchical structure. "By free was meant free from the Pope; for since the Pope was a party in Luther's affair, he should have neither the summoning nor the direction of the Council. It should be called by the Emperor in concert with the Christian princes. By Christian is meant that there were to be present at the

Council not only bishops and clerics but also laymen, who would also take part in its decisions, and that the Council should be conducted "christianly", that is all issues should be judged on the evidence of Scripture alone. Since the quarrel to be settled had broken out in Germany, the Council itself must be held on imperial territory; it was for a similar reason that the Councils of the first centuries were held in the East. It is clear from this that the Nuremberg formula goes far beyond the changes the high and late Middle Ages had brought to the notion of Ecumenical Councils. Viewed in the light of conciliar history, the formula is obviously a revolutionary one."[1]

Emperor Charles V, the Council and the Unity of Christendom

Against this Charles V supported the Church's traditional idea of the Councils. He summarily forbade the German National Council which was due to be held in the Nuremberg Reichstag of 1524 at Speyer. He planned, by means of a General Council convoked by the Pope, to carry out the reform of the Church and overcome the schism as well as restore Church unity. In a sense the Council was the one means he really desired of fulfilling his responsibility for the Empire and Christendom. He writes of himself in his memoirs: "Since 1529, when the Emperor went to Italy for the first time and had a meeting with Pope Clement (VII), he never ceased,

---

[1]H. Jedin, loc. cit.—H. D. Altendorf in his article "Konzile" in RGG, 3rd. Impr., Vol. III, Col. 1803, remarks: "Luther's connection with the destruction of the traditional concept of the Church meant that Protestantism no longer had any room either for the Roman Catholic attitude to the Council or even for the attitude of those who wanted a Council representing the Church in general. The fact that councils could err was not the important point at issue (appeal had, indeed, been made to a Council); even if they did not err— and the decisions of Nicea and Chalcedon remained undisputed despite their unfamiliar terminology—they possessed only a derived authority as interpreters of scripture. Assemblies based on Councils found their way into several Reformation churches, principally of the reformed type, as organs of church administration . . . Ecumenical assemblies are therefore not councils in the traditional Catholic sense because they lack the official charismatic quality."

whenever he saw this Pope or Pope Paul (III), or on all his travels, at all Imperial Councils in Germany, at all other times and under all changing circumstances, either in person or through his ministers, to demand a general council as the sole means of salvation for the ills of Germany and the errors which were spreading throughout Christendom."

In his Bull of Convocation of 22nd May, 1542, Pope Paul III referred to Charles V's numerous efforts to have a General Council held. During the conference the Emperor was represented by his ambassador, Francis of Toledo. Without involving himself at all in matters of dogma he greatly influenced the course of the discussions. To his instigation can be traced, for instance, the parallel discussion of dogma and reform, as well as Paul III's suspension of the Bolognese discussions in 1548; the compulsory attendance of Protestants at the Council of Trent, ordered at the "*armed* Reichstag" at Augsburg in 1547-1548; the re-opening of the Council of Trent on 1st May, 1551 by Julius III and the appearance of the Protestant delegates in the autumn of 1551 and January 1552.

Charles' concern for the Council sprang from his consciousness of being the secular head of Christendom and of his having sovereign claims as protector of the Church in this sphere. His High Chancellor Gattinara wrote to him after his election as Emperor : "Sire, since God has bestowed on you the immense grace of elevating you above all Kings and Princes of Christendom to a sovereignty which before now only Charles the Great, your predecessor, has possessed, you are on the road to a world monarchy, to the coming together of Christendom under one Head". Charles was the last Holy Roman Emperor to be crowned by the pope. His obligation to protect the Church, which he had already taken on by his coronation oath at Aachen on 23rd October, 1520, was consecrated anew by Pope Clement VII on 24th February, 1530, at the coronation in Bologna. His great plan, made early in 1545 in association with

Paul III, of preventing the schism by means of the Council of Trent was already endangered by the transfer of the Council to Bologna. It fell to pieces as a result of a further suspension on 28th April, 1552, made necessary by the conspiracy of princes under the elector Moritz of Saxony. Before Charles V lay the now impossible task of restoring the unity of the Church in the Holy Roman Empire. "All the attempts he had made with unwearying patience to restore the inner unity of the Christian world and to find a basis on which Catholics and Protestants could unite—always with the aim of forming a common front against unbelief—came to nothing, partly through misunderstanding of the real nature of the schism, partly through deeply rooted suspicion, and finally through partisan desires and selfishness which flourished in these critical times as never before".[2] His essentially religious concept of an Emperor prevented him from expressing his recognition of the cleavage in the Church and its faith by entering into a treaty. He therefore left it to his brother, the Roman King Ferdinand, to conclude the "Religious Peace of Augsburg" in 1555, abdicated as King of Spain and Emperor, and retired to private life in his villa near the monastery of St Justus in Estremadura where he died in 1558.

The end of ecclesiastical unity in the Empire was the beginning of the end for the Holy Roman Empire. The abdication of Charles was the conclusion drawn from this knowledge by the last Universal Emperor of the Middle Ages.

Ecclesiological Results of the Council and its indication for the future

The Council of Trent met over three periods—1545-47, 1551-52, and 1562-63. It made decisions about scripture and tradition as sources of faith, original sin and justification, and the sacraments. Its decrees of reform adapted ecclesiastical

---

[2]H. Hantsch, *Die Kaiseridee Karls V.*, Graz 1959, p. 13.

legislation and the care of souls to changed circumstances, removed numerous abuses, and fulfilled as far as was practicable the long frustrated desire of Christendom for Church reform. The first two periods, in their discussion about dogmas of faith, dealt mainly with the view of Luther and Zwingli, but hardly touched Calvin's *Institutio,* which had come out some time before and in 1559 had appeared in its final version. The French bishops took a leading part in the third period, and in the 25th session certain questions arising from the growth of Calvinism in France received their answer in the decree on the veneration of saints, images and relics. The Council was held up twice and in the last period had to struggle against time and bring its discussions to a premature close on the 3rd and 4th December, 1563. And so it was that the Tridentine Council could not deal any further with the main controversial doctrine between Catholics and Protestants, into which all other doctrinal difficulties resolved, namely ecclesiology.

It had already become evident at the Union Conferences in Augsburg in 1530, Leipzig in 1539 and Regensburg in 1541 that the real discords arose out of ecclesiology. This doctrine was, indeed, briefly touched on in connection with scripture and tradition and sacramental teaching, but no special discussion was ever devoted to it. Before Trent controversialists had carried out important preliminary work for the Council but there had not yet been sufficient recognition of how vitally important ecclesiology was for disputations with the Protestants. At first only a few Lutheran propositions which diverged from the Church's teaching were dealt with, along the lines already followed by the Bull *Exsurge Domine* and the University censures. In their sacramental teaching the Fathers at Trent defined Catholic beliefs only so far as was necessary in order to refute the propositions of the reformers. They wisely confined themselves to what was strictly necessary and left it to a later age to fit sacramental teaching into a comprehensive ecclesiological framework. But even during the Council there were already some attempts to arrange the sacraments in relation to the breadth and depth of ecclesiology, such as had been done by Thomas Aquinas, for example, in the third part of the Summa and found expression in the *Decretum pro Armenis*. This decree had already paraphrased the function of each sacrament in the life of the Church as a whole. "The Tridentine Canons made no attempt at all to extend its range of vision. What nowadays is felt to be a regrettable omission is explained by their well-known intention, not of producing a synthesis but of defining individual points. The Sacramental Canons cried out to be set in relation to the Church's essential nature and hierarchical structure. In this context the septenary number of the sacraments and their objects would have been far better grasped, and the depth and breadth of the whole sacramental system made more easily visible."[3]

The importance of the Council of Trent for ecclesiology is not so much in its dealing with particular controversial points inasmuch as they have some bearing on ecclesiology, but rather in the way it was guided, carried through and finally confirmed. The Pope directed all three periods of the Council through his legates who themselves decided which questions were to be discussed. All members of the Council, including the accredited envoys of the Christian princes who had been invited, could indeed make proposals about the acceptance of propositions, but the final decision lay with the papal delegates. The Council took upon itself to define the Church's *depositum fidei* and to prove its basis in Scripture and apostolic tradition. It submitted all its conclusions to the Pope for confirmation, and on 28th January, 1564, Paul IV confirmed all its decrees without exception or any alteration.[4]

---

[3]Denz. 695-702 and H. Jedin, *Geschichte des Konzils von Trient*, II, pp. 332 ff.
[4]The sources give no support to K. Nitzschke's contention that the decisions of the 25th session of the Council of Trent about the acceptance and carrying

By this the Council answered the question both of the hierarchical structure of the Church under the primacy of the Pope and of the relation between the Pope and the General Council. A new impulse was thus given to post-Tridentine theology to develop its ecclesiology with an eye to the acute criticisms of the Reformers. Bellarmine has shown in his "Controversies" that the doctrine of the Church's sacramental structure and hierarchical order lies at the very heart of the disputes and that all controversial doctrines ultimately resolve into it.

A central problem in controversial theology

Is it at all possible to arrive at a principle which will clearly show up the doctrinal contradictions between Catholic and reformed Christendom? Johann Adam Möhler saw this principle in theological anthropology and on this discovery constructed his *Symbolik*. In his *Athanasius* he had already pointed to the Christological structure of the Catholic Church.

out of the Council's decrees "still breathe the conciliaristic spirit throughout". Cf. K. Nitzschke, "Rechtliche Stellung und Vollmacht des Konzils", in: *Im Lichte der Reformation, Jahrbuch des Evangelischen Bundes III*, Göttingen 1960, p. 98. And Nitzschke's other interpretations of the council (*ibid.* pp. 96-98) contradict the wording and the interrelation of the texts as well as the decisions made by the Fathers of the Council, who left it to the Pope to confirm through his legates all decisions reached by the Council. Cf. *Canones et Decreta Concilii Tridentini*, Regensburg 1910, p. 194. H. Jedin replies to the questions brought up by Nitzschke as follows: the Council's decrees undeniably reveal one gap: "The power of the Pope had been one of the principal objects of attack for the reformers ever since the dispute over indulgences. Manuals of controversy such as Eck's Enchiridion had usually devoted considerable space to defending this point of doctrine. But one looks in vain among the Council's decrees on faith for a corresponding decision about the primacy of the Pope and ecclesiological doctrine. Why? The answer must be that in these very matters the unanimity and clarity necessary for a Council definition had not yet been reached on the Catholic side. Gallicanism and episcopalism were still strongly represented at the Council. The dispute, early in 1562, about the *Ius Divinum*, of the residential obligation of bishops, and the Council's great crisis which broke out in the winter of 1562-63 over Chapter 5 and Canon 7 of the *Ordo* decree and paralysed the work of the Council for months, are evidence enough that the time had not yet come for a definition of this matter, however desirable this might have been in itself." H. Jedin, *Katholische Reformation oder Gegenreformation?*, Lucerne 1946, p. 46; cf. also H. Jedin, *Krisis und Wendepunkt des Konzils von Trient 1562-63*, Würzburg 1941, pp. 59ff.

There had been recent attempts in Protestant Christology to establish the basis for the sacramental teaching, the conception of the Church and the doctrine of justification of the Reformers. The aim was to rest the whole structure of reformation doctrine on the place assigned to Christ's humanity in the work of salvation.

Can one go any further? In a penetrating study, written especially with Protestantism in mind, W. H. van de Pol has pointed out two very different ontological and religious outlooks, connecting the first with the Catholic view of God's revelation in the real order and the other with the Protestant revelation in the word. The most profound difference, then, would lie in the fact "that revelation for the Protestant in this world is characteristically a revelation in and through God's word, but for the Catholic a revelation in and through reality."[5]

From this emerge the following main points:

Protestant Christianity understands the Christian dispensation as a promise given in Scripture, the word of God, and as a relationship between the believer and God revealing himself in his word. The Catholic, however, proceeds from the belief that with the Incarnation of the Logos, a real union was formed between God and man in that the Eternal Son of God actually combined in himself a human and a divine nature by the Hypostatic Union. From the Council of Chalcedon's conception of the Incarnation follow the Catholic ideas of the Church and its offices, the sacraments, grace and justification, as well as Mariology and the veneration of the Saints. The entire Catholic conception of Christianity depends on the belief that at the Incarnation the divine order of being entered our earthly one and set up a new supernatural order of being.

On the other hand Protestant Christianity, while retaining the early Christological beliefs, treats the Incarnation as an isolated event in our salvation which does not become a starting

---

[5]W. H. van de Pol, *Das reformatorische Christentum*, Cologne 1956, p. 259.

59

point for constructing a theological system, let alone contribute to any understanding of God's revelation and work of salvation. Revelation here does not mean the setting up of a new order of being in our world but maintains that man is spoken to by God's word and receives salvation as an eschatological promise through his acceptance of this word by faith. From this follow all the other attitudes of the reformers towards grace, justification, merit, the sacraments and, of course, the Church. From this premise it is hardly possible for the Protestant to have any comprehension of what Church and ecclesiastical dignities, priesthood and hierarchy, infallible teaching office and apostolic succession mean in Catholicism.

The reformers themselves saw the doctrine of justification as the main objection to the Catholic Church and this has been the generally accepted opinion among Protestants to this day. But from the fact that the Reformation took *iustificatio per solam fidem* as the hinge of the controversy and the real source of opposition to the Catholic Church, it does not follow that this doctrine, although central to the Reformation, really did form the main contradiction to the Church. Seen from the Catholic viewpoint this is certainly not the case—the essential difference lies in the Church itself as a mystery of faith. What the Church means to the Catholic is inconceivable to the Protestant because of this mistaken premise, which makes the institution of the Church and its teaching office under the guidance of the Holy Spirit appear in a completely different light, rendering its establishment by revelation incomprehensible.

A certain restriction, however, must be made to our description of this premise in regard to Lutheranism, for, although Luther was working in the direction of a theology of the word alone in his major controversial writings, he nonetheless appealed to Catholic tradition in his struggle against over-enthusiastic reformers, particularly to its sacramental teaching about baptism and the Lord's Supper; and by his retention of infant baptism, the Real Presence of Christ in the Lord's Supper and the *manducatio impiorum,* left a door in this theology of "the word alone" open to Catholicism.

From all this it becomes apparent why the real controversial issue between Catholics and Protestants is not the doctrine of justification but ecclesiology. In all discussions of ecclesiological doctrine it is essential to know and make allowances for the Protestant attitude towards the Church both as to its premises and to the conclusions drawn.

Pope John XXIII has frequently made it clear that the impending Council must be an invitation to separated Christians to seek Church unity. He has said that the Council must bring about a strengthening of faith and a renewal of Christian life so that our separated brothers may recognize the Church as their Father's House. To enable separated Christians to see our Church in a new light will largely involve a programme of reform through adaptation to changed circumstances, a renewal of the liturgy, suitable methods of pastoral work and refutation of errors about the Christian view of mankind : a work of renewal, in fact, similar to that undertaken by the Council of Trent in the Chapters *De Reformatione* for the Church of its own time.

Furthermore, to Catholic theology falls the task of answering the questions of our separated fellow-Christians from Scripture and Tradition and the fullness of Catholic truth and to make allowances for the reasons underlying these questions. Pius XII, in his Encyclical *Humani Generis*[6] insisted that theology must have a thorough knowledge of diverging controversial doctrines and at the same time extract whatever truth lies hidden in each one of them and free it from any admixture of error.

This is certainly one of the most important tasks in discus-

[6]Denz. ³¹2308.

sions about ecclesiology, which has been raised to a central position in theological controversy, as the evangelical bishop, Dr. Hanns Lilje pointed out very clearly to the General Synod of Lübeck in October 1959. In the universal search for unity that has led to the setting up of the World Council of the Churches and is causing so many stirrings throughout Christendom, the main question is always about the nature of this unity, and the many different answers stem from the many different concepts of the Church. It is of great importance for the Protestant world to come to realize that an invisible unity is insufficient and that our Lord wants a unity in the same profession of faith, a community of worship centred round the Sacrifice of the Mass, and all under one Ruler. This recognition is not yet by any means universal, but the tendencies which promise most for the future are heading in that direction.

II

The First Vatican Council and its Ecclesiogical Contribution

When Pope Pius IX convoked the Vatican Council on 29th June, 1868, by the Bull *Aeterni Patris,* more than three hundred years had elapsed since the final session of the Council of Trent. There was no longer any Holy Roman Empire, as Francis II, the last Roman Emperor, had laid aside the venerable imperial crown on 6th August, 1806, stating that it was no longer possible for him to fulfil his obligations as Emperor. The concept of Universal Emperor, bound up with that of the Christian community of western peoples, had been kept up in an altered form in the Hapsburg emperors. Admittedly it fitted in with the geographical situation by their defence of Europe against the onslaughts of the Turks, but their function was closely connected with the concept of Universal Emperor. The upheavals of rationalism, the Enlightenment, the French Revolution and secularism had all affected the Church. Christianity and Christian states, such as the Council of Trent had still known them, were no more.

Correspondingly the Vatican Council was even more than the Council of Trent a purely ecclesiastical assembly, and the right to vote was limited in the same way as at Trent. An invitation was sent out to all bishops, even titular bishops, to the heads of all monastic congregations and the generals of religious orders. Pope Pius IX made a reference to the Union Councils of Lyons and Florence in a Brief of 8th September, 1868, inviting also the Bishops of the separated Eastern Churches, but their Patriarchs all declined the invitation. In an open letter of the 13th September, 1868, the Pope invited "all Protestants and non-Catholics" to return to Christ's one flock. Apart from a few favourable letters and publications, particularly in England, nothing but refusals were given by Protestants in Germany, France, Switzerland and Holland as well as the United States. The Council, therefore, could not become a Union Council. Pius IX was quite prepared to invite Protestant observers to the Council's discussions. He wrote a letter to Archbishop Manning of Westminster "in which he made clear his desire for the reunion of Protestants with the Catholic Church as well as his intention of giving them a good opportunity to bring forward their doctrines and their reasons for them. Even if they were not in a position to do this themselves during the sessions of the Council, they would most certainly find men of their own choosing, skilled in theology, to whom they could present their arguments for examination and discussion. Lastly he expressed his wish that many might be present at the Council for this purpose".[7] It was hoped in many Protestant circles that the Vatican Council would lay the foundations for a future reunion. But it was also realized that Christendom—in the new sense of the word—would remain divided indefinitely.

The Council of Trent had invited the Emperor, the King of France and all Christian princes to take part. During the preparations for the Vatican Council this problem had to be considered in the light of a completely altered situation. Granderath writes: "The relation of Church and State has so changed in our times that we can scarcely imagine the close mutual relation in which the two societies stood to one another, and find it difficult to think of an emperor or king sitting at the same Council with bishops". All the same, the cardinals were very doubtful about passing over the princes, for this would mean "abandoning an ancient tradition". But "the relation of Church and State had indeed become completely different". It was finally thought sufficient to send a request to the princes not to put any obstacles in the way of the participation of the bishops and ask them in general terms for their co-operation. The princes and their envoys were expressly invited to attend in person the solemn sessions and also the voting, in an honorary capacity as guests and observers.[8]

While the Council of Trent had to start its work with almost no preparation at all, the Vatican Council was very carefully planned and prepared. Pius IX had already on 6th December, 1864, sought the favourable opinion of twenty-one Cardinals of the Curia about the opportuneness of holding a General Council. Cardinal Reisach had pointed out in his reply that the Council of Trent had not expressly refuted the basic error of the reformers, their rejection of a hierarchic Church

[7]Th. Granderath, *Geschichte des Vatikanischen Konzils*, Vol. I, Freiburg in Breisgau 1903, p. 334.
[8]*Ibid.*, pp. 129-132.

and its infallible teaching authority. "The problem about the Church, repeatedly discussed and contested since the days of Boniface VIII and Marsiglio of Padua, still remained."[9] When the Council was opened the five preparatory sub-committees had already for a year been carrying out very detailed preliminary work, and had the Council's agenda complete and published.

The Dogmatic Constitution of Catholic Faith

The twentieth General Council sat from 8th December, 1869 to 18th July, 1870, and in the third session of 24th April, 1870, decreed the four Chapters and eighteen Canons of the Dogmatic Constitution of Faith. This Constitution condemned rationalism, which denied or misinterpreted supernatural revelation, and also fideism, which rejected any knowledge of God by unaided reason. Kant had wanted to salvage our knowledge of God's existence from its wreck in the Enlightenment and place it on the level of reason (Vernunft). He denied the possibility of knowledge of God by our own powers in order to free it from the secularizing influence of deism and affirmed the freedom of the will, the immortality of the soul and the existence of God as postulates of the practical reason. This was a denial of the basis of theology. The Vatican Council, while condemning this denial of our real knowledge of God as erroneous, defended the connection between our belief and our powers of knowledge : man can know the existence of God as Creator and Lord of the moral order by the natural light of reason; likewise he can know the fact of revelation, the mysteries of which, even after his acceptance of them through faith aided by grace, never become fully grasped and remain veiled as in darkness.[10]

---

[9]H. Jedin, *Ecumenical Councils in the Catholic Church*, *loc. cit.*, For the preparation cf. Th. Granderath, *loc. cit.*, pp. 20-45; 46-56; 62-82; 389-453.
[10]Denz. 1785-1799. For Kant's philosophy cf.: *Kant und die Scholastik heute*, ed. by Joh. B. Lotz (Pullacher Philosophische Forschungen, Vol. I), Pullach, Munich, 1955.

The history of events leading up to the Dogmatic Constitution has been very thoroughly described by Granderath and Cuthbert Butler. The first draft, which was distributed on 10th December, 1869, came up against very strong criticism. The general objection was to the vague and abstract language, but it was also the opinion that the draft did not meet contemporary requirements. The French theologian, Charles Gay of Poitiers, summed up the general discontent in these words: the draft "deals too much with errors which are scarcely known outside the Schools, and too little with those which confuse the minds of men and constitute a danger to society". Not only the presidents of the Council and the theologians but also the Pope were surprised by this almost unanimous rejection. The *Deputatio de fide,* led by Cardinal Bilio, proceeded straightway with the revision. It agreed unanimously that the draft should be shortened and more clearly worded, the scholastic terminology avoided as much as possible and any complicated turn of phrase eliminated; and also that any restriction on the freedom of admissible scholastic opinions should be avoided.

The discussion of this first draft has surprising parallels with the discussion of the first draft of the decree on justification at the Council of Trent. Then also the Fathers of the Council chastized the longwinded official language, couched in the jargon of scholastic theology, which was put before them on 24th July, 1546; it, too, was subsequently given a thorough revision.

The revision of the Vatican draft was entrusted to Archbishop Dechamps of Malines, Bishop Pie of Poitiers and Bishop Martin of Paderborn. Bishop Konrad Martin of Paderborn was given the work of drawing up the new text. Butler calls him a learned theologian, an agreeable controversialist and a truly apostolic Bishop. Martin took on two theologians to help him, the German Jesuit, Fr. Kleutgen, and the French theologian

66

already mentioned, Charles Gay. On 1st March, 1870, the Bishop of Paderborn was already able to lay the result of his labours before the Deputation. He had divided the draft into two parts. The first dealt with the fundamental truths of God as Creator, revelation, faith and the relation of faith to reason. The second part, which was never actually discussed, dealt with particular Christian doctrines : the most Holy Trinity, the creation of man and human nature, the graces bestowed on the first human being, the fall, the mystery of the Incarnation and the graces of redemption.

Charles Gay had written a long preface to the draft in which rationalism, pantheism, materialism and atheism were so closely linked to Protestantism as to make it seem that Protestantism, by its rejection of any teaching authority and its substitution of the principle of *scriptura sola* had led to subjectivism, to the abandonment of inspired scripture and ultimately to rationalism. On 22nd March, 1870, Bishop Strossmayer reacted against this preface in a passionate speech, into which he unfortunately drew the question of the "moral unanimity" of the Council's decisions, which was utterly irrelevant. On the following day Bishop Meignan of Chalons very clearly and reasonably stressed that the preface should avoid any appearance of making Protestantism the source of such errors as pantheism and materialism, which had existed long before the advent of Protestantism. The offending passages were dropped from the final text approved on 29th March. In addition a number of gratuitously offensive expressions were struck out. It is worthy of note that these changes and omissions marked a return to the draft which Konrad Martin had originally submitted to the Deputation. Martin's draft was, furthermore, a masterpiece of clear exposition and beautiful, easily understood Latin.

The Pope as successor of the Prince of Apostles and the Bishops
    as successors of the Apostles

On 3rd June, 1870, there began the special discussion about
the Primacy of the Pope. Butler rightly says that, though the
question of Papal Infallibility raised most of the storms at that
time, the matter of the Primacy as defined in the third Chapter
of the Dogmatic Constitution of 18th July, 1870, provided non-
Catholics of all denominations with much greater difficulties
and stumbling-blocks in the way of a united Christendom in
communion with the Apostolic Chair in Rome, which nowadays more than ever is the dream and goal of the prayer and
efforts of countless men of good will who still remain outside
this communion.

The comments made by the bishops about the doctrine of
primacy, as brought out so strongly in the original draft on the
Church, prove that none of the bishops questioned the Primacy
either in its full extent or its implications. The critical comments
only show that a collective representation of Catholic ecclesiological doctrine cannot simply deal with the pope and the
Church, but must also bring in the hierarchy as a whole, the
episcopacy, the Holy Office and the General Councils. Because
of this many bishops wished a new chapter to be included in
the draft defining Catholic doctrine about the status, jurisdiction, rights, authority and duties of bishops. They particularly
urged it to be made clear that bishops are not, by virtue of the
"immediate and ordinary" jurisdiction of the pope in all
bishoprics, mere vicars or delegates of the pope, but rather
exercise "ordinary and immediate" jurisdiction in their own
dioceses. Archbishop Melchers of Cologne declared: "The
pope undoubtedly has full and supreme power over the whole
Church and every part of it; this should nonetheless be exercised having regard to the rights of bishops. The jurisdiction
of bishops is immediate and ordinary, conferred by God, for
each to use in his own diocese; but it is subordinated to the

pope in Rome in such a way that his supreme power of jurisdiction over every individual part of the whole Church is also immediate and ordinary.

As part of the task laid on him by the Deputation, Joseph Kleutgen composed a new *Schema Constitutionis dogmaticae secundae de Ecclesia Christi secundum reverendissimorum animadversiones reformatum*. This draft was first published in Volume 53 of Mansi's *Collectio Conciliorum* from the author's own manuscript. The first three chapters are devoted to the divine institution of the Church, the Church as *coetus fidelium* and the authority of the Church based on Christ's command—and chapter four to the ecclesiastical hierarchy. Chapter four is in three parts : the first part is a declaration of the pre-eminence of bishops over priests in virtue of their *potestas ordinandi* and *potestas iurisdictionis*. Secondly the role of bishops in instructing and guiding the whole Church is shown in the following words :

"But bishops also have a share in the supreme office of teaching and guiding the whole Church. For it is evident that the full power of binding and loosing which was given to Peter alone was also given to the group of apostles who were so closely associated with the Head of the Church. Our Lord indeed affirmed 'Amen, I say to you, whatsoever you shall bind upon earth shall be bound also in heaven; and whatever you shall loose upon earth shall be loosed also in heaven.' (Matt. 18 : 18). And so from the Church's beginning the conclusions and ordinances of ecumenical councils have rightly been accepted by the faithful with the greatest reverence as the utterances of God and the decisions of the Holy Ghost."

In the third part of chapter four the unity of the bishops and their subordination to the pope is discussed. At the end it is explicitly said that it is for the pope not only to convoke and terminate a council but also to guide and confirm it.

Kleutgen's draft, to which a certain measure of authority

is not to be denied, had a solid basis given it by its author, both in its whole conception and its individual chapters—it included yet another six chapters. The Deputation, however, did not give its full ratification to the draft and did not submit it for further discussion. The matter contained in the fourth chapter of the *Schema constitutionis dogmaticae secundae* came into its own in the third chapter of the *constitutio dogmatica prima de Ecclesia Christi*. It was due to Cardinal Rauscher of Vienna and Bishop Freppel of Angers that the relation of papal primacy to the jurisdiction of bishops was made clear by this explanatory supplement which was incorporated in the final version of chapter three.

But, as is well known, greater difficulties were provided by the final version of the fourth chapter "of the infallible teaching office of the Pope in Rome". After long debates on the original text which was issued to the Fathers of the Council on 6th March, 1870, Bishop Konrad Martin of Paderborn as a member of the Deputation submitted an entirely new version of the whole chapter on the 30th June, together with a long supplement which actually stated the underlying reasons for the final form which this supplement took. The records of the deputation prove that even the final formula for the definition of infallibility (Denz. 1839) can be traced back to a formula first suggested by Bishop Martin which was further worked on by the theologians Franzelin and Schrader.

In the fourth session of 18th July, 1870, the Dogmatic Constitution of the primacy and infallibility of the Pope was decided on. Since the Council was obliged by pressure of outside events to bring its conferences to an early conclusion, the body of doctrines about the Church was not put forward for discussion. Although the majority regretted this postponement at the time, it was perhaps providential, for in any case modern theology has at its disposal a great deal of exegetical and patristic literature as well as works of reference which were not available during the Vatican Council. Furthermore we now have a series of papal pronouncements which fortunately can complete the Vatican definitions of papal primacy and infallibility and lay the foundations for a full exposition of the nature of the Church, and especially of the office of bishops. Thus it is now possible to develop a theology of the episcopacy and the *Collegium apostolicum episcoporum* with the aid of the Vatican Council, Leo XIII's encyclical *Satis cognitum* of 29th June, 1896, and the encyclical *Mystici corporis,* all with the guarantee given by the successor of Peter.[11] The definition of the Pope's primacy and infallibility is far from being a hindrance to the development of a theological study of the episcopacy; on the contary, this definition, with its emphasis on the unchanging structure of the Church and on the principle which unites all bishops, was alone able to lay the way open for a thorough study of the episcopacy and the *Collegium apostolicum episcoporum* in the light of Holy Scripture and the traditions of both East and West. Pius XII, in his encyclical *Fidei Donum,* stressed that by virtue of the apostolic succession the whole episcopacy under the governance of the Pope is responsible as a body for the universal mission of the Church.

The definition of the Pope's primacy of jurisdiction and infallibility in the exercise of the supreme teaching office has removed the obstacles which have so long stood in the way of the development of ecclesiology. Even during the last period of the Council of Trent the absence of this definition was the reason why the Council became so seriously delayed for months on end on the question of a bishop's obligation of residence. Gallicanism and Febronianism during the last few centuries have repeatedly endangered the unity of the Church and

---

[11]Denz. 1821. For the whole cf. the abundant references to the sources in H. Schauf, "De corpore Christi mystico sive de Ecclesia Christi Theses" in: *Die Ekklesiologie des Konzilstheologen Clemens Schrader,* Freiburg 1959.

hindered the development of ecclesiology. But this study gained an undreamt-of impetus after the Vatican Council. Once the Apostolic Chair had been declared the criterion of unity it was possible to work out this thorough exposition which has found its officially confirmed expression in Pope Pius XII's encyclical *Mystici Corporis*.

The Vatican Council rejected the opinion "that the authority of the Supreme Pontiff detracts from the ordinary immediate power of episcopal jurisdiction by which bishops, appointed by the Holy Ghost as true shepherds, feed and guide the flocks entrusted to their care, each one his own; but rather this is protected, strengthened and defended by the Supreme Universal Pastor".[12]

Leo XIII developed this idea still further in his encyclical *Satis cognitum* of 29th June, 1896: "Though the authority of St Peter and his successors is the fullest and highest, it must not be thought to be the only one. For He himself who destined St Peter for the foundation of the Church, chose also the twelve . . ., whom he named apostles. Just as the authority of St Peter must continue in the Church, so too do the bishops, as successors of the apostles, inherit the power of Orders, so that the episcopate belongs necessarily to the inner constitution of the Church. Though they do not possess full, universal and supreme authority, yet they are not just representatives of the Pope of Rome, for they possess their own authority, and are called, in the fullest sense of the words, shepherds in virtue of their Order of the people committed to them".[13]

---

[12]Denz. 1828. For the basis in scripture and the Fathers cf. Jean Colson, "Evangélisation et collégialité apostolique", in *Nouvelle Revue Théologique*, Vol. 82, 1960, pp. 349-372.
[13]ASS XXVIII (1896), 732. (Cf. Neuner-Roos, *Der Glaube der Kirche*, 5th ed., Regensburg 1958), No. 388a: Kollektiverklärung des deutschen Episkopates und ihre Billigung durch Pius IX. (1875). This document is important for the question of the relation between papal and episcopal authority. After the Vatican Council Bismarck had declared in a communiqué of 14th May, 1872 that the bishops had been degraded by the immediate and

Pope and Bishops united in the Ecumenical Council

What this means for the status of bishops at a General Council has been set forth by Bishop Zinelli of Treviso, the spokesman of the *Deputatio de fide* of the Vatican Council. He said : "If we consider the sources of revelation, it becomes clear that a full and supreme authority in the Church was given to Peter and his successors, in such a way that it cannot be limited by any human power set over it. Natural and divine law are its only boundaries. Many Fathers of the Council may ask : Does not this authority similarly reside also to the same extent in the Ecumenical Council? Did not Christ promise all the Apostles that he would be with them? Did he not say to all the Apostles : 'What you shall bind on earth shall be bound in Heaven; and what you shall loose on earth shall be loosened in Heaven? Did he not make other pronouncements which make it clear that he wished to bestow the highest authority possible on his Church? . . . We affirm that when we are assembled in the Ecumenical Council as bishops united with our Head, there resides in us the Church's fullness of power over the faithful. The Bishops assembled in the Ecumenical Council with their Head, who in this case represent the whole Church, or dispersed but still united with their head, who in this case form the Church itself (*in quo casu sunt ipsa Ecclesia*), truly possess the fullness of authority." These two supreme powers, adds Zinelli, are, nonetheless, not distinct and separate from one another. "On the contrary we declare that the 'plena et suprema potestas' (full and highest power) resides in the same way in the Head joined to its members, i.e., in the Pope with

universal primacy of jurisdiction of the Pope to mere functionaries and officials. Against this the German episcopacy composed a collective statement in January and February, 1875. In an Apostolic Letter of 2nd March, 1875, Pius IX approved this teaching of the German hierarchy in an unusually solemn form, saying: "Your statement reproduces the genuine Catholic doctrine, which is also that of the Holy Council and of this Holy Chair, defends it with illuminating and irrefutable reasons and it explains it so clearly as to make it comprehensible to any just man and to avoid any innovation in the (conciliar) definitions which have been impugned".

the Bishops. .... As the *plena et suprema potestas* cannot truly exist in a body separated from its head, individual bishops, however many of them there may be, cannot exercise the *plena et suprema potestas* without their Head. On the other hand the Pope, as Head, can exercise his supreme authority, even independently of the co-operation of the bishops."[4]

Likewise Canon 218 of the Codex of Canon Law says that the Pope, as the successor of St Peter, possesses the *plenam potestatem iurisdictionis in universam Ecclesiam,* and Canon 228 says: *Concilium Oecumenicum suprema pollet in universam Ecclesiam potestate.*

The Vatican Council defined that the *ex cathedra* pronouncements of the Pope "are unalterable in their own right, not by the assent of the Church".[15] This means that the assent of the bishops is neither the cause nor the necessary condition of the infallibility of *ex cathedra* pronouncements. The basis of infallibility is the assistance of the Holy Ghost, not the assent of the bishops or the Church as a whole.

But the Vatican Council did not in any way declare itself against the Pope holding discussions with the Bishops before-

---

[14]*Collectio Lacensis,* (Friburgi Brisgoviae 1890): "Acta et Decreta Concilii Vaticani," cols. 357-358; cf. Th. Granderath, *Geschichte des Vatikanischen Konzils* Vol. III (Freiburg in Breisgau, 1906), pp. 363-364; P. Umberto Betti, O.F.M., "Natura e portata del Primato del Romano Pontefice secondo il Concilio Vaticano", in: *Antonianum,* Vol. XXXIV (1959), pp. 161-244; 369-408. Cf. also C. Butler, *loc. cit.* pp. 308-310. Butler proves (pp. 337-339) that the final formula of the definition of Papal Infallibility can be traced to Bishop Konrad Martin of Paderborn. Cf. *Collectio Lacensis, loc. cit.,* cols. 1683d, 1684a-b, 1700b, 1701a.—R. Aubert, making use of sources up to now in part unedited, proves that Bishop Martin was from the beginning a decided supporter of the definition of Papal Infallibility and that he managed to have himself put forward for the task of systematically examining the comments made against the first draft of 6th March, 1870, and considering the points in their favour. R. Aubert, "Documents concernant le tiers parti au Concile du Vatican", in: *Abhandlungen über Theologie und Kirche, Festschrift für Karl Adam,* Düsseldorf, 1952, pp. 242-243, p. 257, n. 13. R. Aubert on p. 255 concludes: La définition qui fut solonnellement approuvée le 18 juillet, était comme on sait, singulièrement plus nuancée que le texte primitif et donnait au fond satisfaction aux légitimes exigences de la grande majorité des évêques: c'est du reste ce qui explique que tous les opposants finirent par s'y soumettre, une fois qu'ils se furent éloignés du feu de la bataille.

[15]Denz. 1839.

74

hand, but expressly stated: "The Roman Bishops have, in accordance with the demands of time and situation, by the convocation of General Councils or by investigation into the opinion of the Church all over the world, by Particular Synods or by other means given by Divine Providence, declared as firm doctrine whatever they have unanimously agreed on with God's aid as well as by consulting Holy Scripture and Apostolic Traditions".[16] The pope receives no new revelation, he defines what, after careful examination of the sources of faith, he sees to be "in accordance with Holy Scripture and Apostolic Tradition".[17] Consultation with the Bishops is,[18] according to the Vatican Council's pronouncements about the Church's teaching office, the first and foremost help in preparing a definition. Thus we also see that Pius IX consulted the Bishops before defining the dogma of the Immaculate Conception. Pius XII, in his letter *Deiparae Virginis Mariae,* enquired of all Catholic Bishops the world over whether in their view the Blessed Virgin's bodily assumption into Heaven could be put forward and defined as a dogma and whether they, together with their clergy and their faithful, wished for this. In the Apostolical Constitution, *Munificentissimus Deus,* Pius XII emphatically pointed to the value as a testimony and the power as a proof such a doctrinal pronouncement by the whole hierarchy would have and would show forth "the unanimous doctrine of the Church's teaching office and the unanimous faith of Christian people guided and supported by this teaching office."[19]

Looking back on the history of the twenty great Church assemblies we can discern the changing appearance of the

---

[16]Denz. 1836.
[17]Denz. 1836.
[18]Denz. 1792, 1821, 1836.
[19]Pii Papae XII Constitutio Apostolica *Munificentissimus Deus,* Roma, 1950, p. 6.

Councils. Only the Bishops as successors of the Apostles possess a *ius divinum*, independent of the Canon Law in force at any given period, to have an active voice in the Council. For only the Bishops who have jurisdiction, together with the Pope as their centre of unity,[20] form the teaching Church and represent the Apostolic College. Church Law can, with regard to privileges and customs, grant others a place in the Council and accord them a deliberative function (e.g., Titular Bishops) or a consultative one (e.g., theologians). The changing appearance of the ecumenical council is accounted for by alterations in ordinary Ecclesiastical Law brought about by the needs of the age, while its permanent fundamental structure is a result of the perpetual *ius divinum* of the Bishops united with the Pope. The *Codex Iuris Canonici* has legally formulated the modern pattern of the Council in connection with Trent and particularly with the Vatican Council.[21] According to this the following are invited to the Council and possess a right to take part in the discussions :

1. Cardinals, even if they are not bishops.
2. Patriarchs, Primates, Archbishops and residential Bishops, even if they have not yet been consecrated. In this event the bishops are already possessed of jurisdiction, and their pastoral responsibility entitles them to take part.
3. Abbots or Prelates *nullius* exercising jurisdiction over a limited number of the faithful.
4. Mitred Abbots and generals of orders or congregations of monasteries and the generals of exempt orders of clerics, but not those of other orders unless some other provision is made in the Decree of Convocation.
5. Titular bishops also can be invited to a Council and take part in the deliberations unless some other provision is expressly made at the convocation. Titular bishops, for instance auxiliary

---

[20]Denz. 1821.
[21]*C.J.C.*, can. 223. cf. Th. Granderath, *loc. cit.*, Vol. I, pp. 83-132.

bishops, have indeed been consecrated but have no episcopal jurisdiction. These were invited to take part in the deliberations at the Vatican Council.

6. If theologians and canonists are invited to the Council they have no voice in the deliberations but only a consultative capacity.

Any of those invited who is unable to attend in person must send a procurator who can attend the session without a right to vote, and add his signature to the decrees at the end.[22]

The right to convoke an Ecumenical Council is the Pope's alone; he presides over the conferences in person or through his legates and decides on the agenda and the subjects to be discussed. The Fathers of the Council can add other questions to those submitted by the Pope, which must first be accepted by the President of the Council. The Pope can transfer, suspend and terminate the Council; he must confirm the decisions in order to make them valid and binding.[23]

These norms provide us with the basic structure of a future council, which is of great importance for the progress of the discussions. Both ecclesiology and the particular form of the Council are to some extent reflected in the agenda.[24]

---

[22]Can. 224.
[23]Can. 222, 226.
[24]Cf. H. Jedin, "Die Geschäftsordnungen der beiden letzten ökumenischen Konzilien in ekklesiologischer Sicht," in: *Catholica*, Vol. 14, 1960, pp. 105-118; for the Tridentine agenda: H. Jedin, *Geschichte des Konzils von Trient, loc. cit.*, Vol. I, pp. 9-41; p. 53; pp. 91-96. For the Vatican Council: Th. Granderath, *loc. cit.*, Vol. I, pp. 389-421; Vol. II, pp. 38-61: *Die Konzilsordnung und die Aufnahme derselben.*

CHAPTER FIVE

Legacy from the Past:
Mandate for the Present

WITH the ending of the Vatican Council and the solemn definition of papal infallibility in teaching, some were of the opinion that General Councils had become unnecessary. Döllinger, during his period of allegiance to the "Old Catholic" cause, often expressed the view that the Vatican definition of the primacy and infallibility of the pope would lessen the importance of bishops as successors of the apostles, to the point of making their office superfluous and General Councils a thing of the past. Among Catholics also the opinion could be found that the importance of General Councils was considerably lessened. "What," they asked, "was the need for General Councils, since the pope as supreme teacher of the Church *ex cathedra* is endowed with the infallibility Christ promised to the Church as a whole?"

Hence the surprise when Pope John, on the 25th January, 1959, announced a new General Council. Between the last two Councils, of Trent (1545-1563) and of the Vatican (1869-1870), there was an interval of more than 300 years. Yet barely ninety years after the Vatican, a new Council has been announced.

Closely connected with the doubts about the value of a

General Council after the Vatican is the question of the relation of the pope to a Council.

I

The Pope and the Council

An Ecumenical or General Council is a solemn assembly, called by the pope, of the bishops of the Catholic world, to consider and decide, under the presidency of the pope, matters concerning the whole of Christendom. An Ecumenical Council is always a universal Council; the terms have the same meaning. To be "ecumenical" in the full sense, a Council must be universal as to its summoning, its execution and its power. In the traditional terminology, a Council is ecumenical and universal only if it is juridically representative, the authoritative organ, of the whole Church. It cannot be representative of that apart from the pope, without whom the Church would be a visible body with no visible head, an *acephalic* Church.

The necessity of a visible head cannot be gainsaid on the ground that, even without the pope, the Council has a head, namely Christ. Christ is the invisible Head of the whole Church. This he is in virtue of his fullness of power, and from him grace flows into men, who are thereby made righteous before God. But the pope, by the will of Christ as witnessed by the New Testament, is Christ's visible representative as to "the external government of the members of the Church", as possessing the office of supreme shepherd and teacher,[1] not through any fullness of power of his own, but as commissioned by Christ, and so he is the visible head of the Church, without whom the Council cannot be truly ecumenical.

---

[1] Aquinas, *Summa Theologica*, III, qu. 8 art. 6.

EC 4

Since its separation from Rome, the Orthodox Church has never seriously attempted to call an Ecumenical Council. Many theologians of the Eastern Church hold that the Orthodox Churches alone could not summon an Ecumenical Council, since they are not the universal Church, but only a part of it. Others are of the opinion that the want of visible unity can be made up for by the invisible bond with Christ as Head of the Church. But we cannot accept this; Christ willed a visible unity of all who believe in him.

Thus the participation of the pope is indispensable for a Council to be ecumenical; and, at the same time, it is often sufficient in order to complete what may be lacking in ecumenicity, for papal participation is a guarantee of the universal validity of Conciliar decisions. That is why many Councils can only be considered ecumenical as to a part of their decisions, since papal co-operation and sanction was lacking to the rest.[2]

II

When does a Council become Ecumenical?

A Council is ecumenical at the moment of its summons, if all the bishops of the Catholic world have been officially invited. For it also to be ecumenical from the beginning of its sessions the invitations must have reached their destinations and been answered from every part of the Church. It is, in practice, unavoidable for some of the bishops to be prevented from attending. Clearly, then, the ecumenical character of the Council cannot depend on the actual participation of all, or nearly all, the bishops. Nor is it necessary for the majority of bishops to be present. Further, it cannot be required that every

---

[2] Cf. *Codex jur. can.*, canons 222-229, also J. Forget, *op. cit.*, col. 602-607.

country or nation should be actually represented by its own bishop. As a proof that a majority of bishops is not necessary, we can instance the Council of Trent, which opened, on 13th December, 1545, with four cardinals, four archbishops (of Aix, Palermo, Upsala, Armagh—from four different nations), and twenty-one bishops, three quarters of them Italian, two Spaniards, an Englishman and a German. In addition, there were the Generals of the Franciscan Observants, Franciscan Conventuals, Augustinian Hermits, Carmelites and Servites. The Catholic diocesan bishops at the time numbered more than five hundred, not including the English, Scandinavian and German bishops who had gone over to the Reformation; so the number present at the opening was indeed modest. Nonetheless, the Council of Trent is held ecumenical from its beginning on 13th December, 1545. It makes no difference that the German bishops, though invited, were almost wholly absent. They have been severely blamed for this on the ground that they failed to see the importance of the Council and were more concerned for their temporal authority and possessions than for their spiritual duty to attend the Council. But in justice we ought to consider the difficulties of their position. In the tension prevailing just before the Schmalkaldic war, their absence from home might well have induced the neighbouring Protestant rulers to seize their bishoprics, which would then have been lost to the Catholic faith.

How many must be present as a minimum for a Council to be ecumenical? No simple and conclusive answer is given either by theologians or Canon Law. We can, however, formulate some general rules.

After all the bishops and those entitled have been invited, voting members from various countries must assemble, under the direction of the proper authority, in such a number that it can be truly said, having regard to the conditions of the time, that the entire Church is represented. In case of doubt whether a Council be ecumenical, it belongs to the Church's teaching authority to decide the question as one of dogmatic fact (*factum dogmaticum*). An authoritative decision of the kind cannot make ecumenical what was not already such, but it can infallibly settle that a Council was really ecumenical. Further, it can give ecumenical validity to a Council which was not ecumenical at the time of its meeting. For instance, the eastern bishops were alone invited to the first Council of Constantinople (381); and the second (553) was, at first, only an eastern one. But both received ecumenical status through subsequent ratification by the pope and agreement of the western Church.

At all three periods of the Council of Trent, Protestants of all kinds were officially invited. The Schmalkalders refused to take part, and so the Protestants were entirely unrepresented in the first period (1545-1547). In the course of the second period (1551-1552), there were present Protestant emissaries from Brandenburg, Württemburg and Saxony, at the end of 1551 and on 9th January, 1552. These, however, not content with demanding that all dogmatic decisions should be postponed till the arrival of their own theologians, which was granted, required also that the Council's former decisions should be reconsidered, that the Catholic bishops should be released from their oath of fidelity to the pope, and that the Council should assert its superiority to the pope. These demands were unacceptable, being at variance with the Church's traditional conception of ecumenical councils. The tension which resulted threatened a cessation of the proceedings. The rebellion of the princes against Charles V compelled the Council to be suspended on 28th April, 1552. But the absence of the Protestants, who had been granted letters of safe-conduct and guaranteed full freedom of speech, could not prevent the Council being ecumenical.

III

Papal Infallibility does not make Councils Superfluous

We turn now to the question asked in the beginning. The Vatican definition has made no change in the importance of General Councils. The popes have always given doctrinal decisions on their authority as supreme teachers. Further, Councils in the early age of the Church, as those of Ephesus and Chalcedon, clearly stated that their intention was to give effect to a previous papal decision on doctrine. It follows that Councils are not absolutely necessary, and that the Church, as in the first centuries, can exist without them. They cannot be shown to be necessary either from Scripture or from Tradition. And it is a matter of history that, as a rule, it was the Eastern Roman emperor, rather than the pope or bishops, who initiated the first Councils.

This does not alter the fact that Councils are extremely useful, and often almost morally necessary. No other means was so adapted for ending the Great Schism as a General Council. The way to carry out a reform of the whole Church in the sixteenth century, and to decide the questions raised by the Reformation, was, to Catholics and, in principle, to most Protestants, the calling of a general Council; and the gigantic task was, in fact, performed by the Council of Trent.

To appreciate fully the importance of an ecumenical Council, we must bear in mind the real nature of the infallibility of the pope and of the episcopate united with him. Infallibility does not involve any new revelation, and infallible teaching is not necessarily inspired. It is rather a matter of simple assistance, by which God preserves his Church and her head from error in formal decisions on faith and morals. Normally, these decisions presuppose human endeavour, reflexion, study of sources and theological reasoning. If the pope takes it on himself to decide matters of faith or to propound reforms, doubtless he will be kept from error in teaching by divine assistance. But this does not mean that he necessarily chooses the best way of expressing these doctrines or the reforms best suited to the given circumstances. The collaboration of the bishops in a Council brings out many aspects the pope might have overlooked. The Council of Chalcedon provides us with a good example. Pope Leo had, in his letter to Flavian, expounded the mystery of the Incarnation in opposition to the Monophysites and Nestorians, and the Fathers of Chalcedon solemnly declared their acceptance. But some eastern bishops thought that some of the expressions in the letter took insufficient account of the different terminology of the Eastern Church. They worked out a new formulation of the dogma, which, in contrast to the floridity of the papal letter, was terse and precise in terms unfamiliar to Rome and the West, and removed any possibility of misinterpretation. There resulted a masterpiece of clearness and accuracy which effectively prevented the Monophysites accusing the Council of Nestorianism.

Further examples are the enormous work done by the bishops and theologians at Trent and the Vatican. This work of reason enlightened by faith, together with hard and fruitful study and evaluation of sources, alone made possible the final form of the Conciliar decrees.

Ecumenical Councils are a wonderful demonstration of Catholic unity in their formal pronouncements by the whole episcopate, preceded by the most careful deliberation and informed by thorough theological research. They are the most appropriate means of proclaiming revealed truth in an impressive manner and refuting error. Being the work of the Church as a whole, their decisions impress men more strongly than those coming from the Holy See alone, and they have a like authority. The bishops who take part in a Council are best fitted to decide on doctrine, after collaborating to that end; they will be the more zealous in carrying out the reforms they have themselves decided. Their deliberations give them a deeper understanding of theological questions, which will make more fruitful the discharge of their teaching office.

In a lecture delivered in August 1960, Cardinal Montini said that the pope's decision to call a Council amounted to a refutation of the opinion, hitherto seemingly not unjustified, that Councils are, as it were, merely tolerated by the popes. The opinion too that the proclamation of papal infallibility at the first Vatican Council would bring about the end of Councils cannot now be sustained.[3]

IV

The Ecumenical Council as Representative of the Entire Church

Press articles on the Council show the different meanings given to the word "ecumenical", according as it is used by Protestant, Orthodox or Catholic writers, and that they are bound up with very different conceptions in the field of theology and canon law. I will speak here only of the fundamental Catholic idea of a Council, without discussing the

---

[3] Cf. the account given in *Kath. Nachrichten-Agentur* No. 184, 18th August, 1960.

various types of Council found in history nor any particular details of Church history.

An Ecumenical Council is a solemn assembly of all bishops throughout the world to discuss, in union with the bishop of Rome, questions which concern the whole of Christendom. To be truly ecumenical certain conditions must be fulfilled as regards its summoning, execution and authority.

1. The summoning: How do the bishops united with the pope represent the whole Church?

A Council is ecumenical in its summoning, if all the bishops of the Catholic world have been officially invited. By divine law, all bishops possessing actual jurisdiction in a definite territory must be invited. The reason is that the bishops, as successors of the apostles, form, with the pope, the teaching body of the Church, which represents the highest ecclesiastical authority. By the customary law of the Church now in force, the class of those to be invited has been widened, to include holders of ecclesiastical offices bearing quasi-episcopal jurisdiction. In addition, all titular bishops were invited to the Vatican Council, since these possess, by their consecration, all that befits them to receive jurisdiction.[4]

The question may be asked: How are the laity represented at a Council? Pope John XXIII, in an address referring to the Roman diocesan synod, expressly stated that "the laity are not directly summoned to take part in the synod". They are represented through their bishops. The teaching body of the Church is in intimate union with the whole body of the faithful. Together with them the bishops form an organic body that preserves and gives expression to Christian truth; this body is the Church. Those who teach the faith are themselves believers and confessors of that faith; and to it all believers testify by their profession and their lives. The Holy Spirit, who animates and

---

[4] Cf. Th. Granderath, *loc. cit.* pp. 84-132.

guides the teaching body, also animates and guides all believers directly and inwardly in virtue of the grace of Baptism, and empowers them to witness actively to Christian truth. It is not witnessed to exclusively by the official, authentic and authoritative teaching of the Bishops, but also by the universal and continuous confessing of the faithful. The whole body of the faithful has an important function in preserving and developing the faith. In Baptism and Confirmation they have received the Holy Spirit, who works in them actively. The Spirit operates through his gifts in every baptised person in the state of grace. The gifts of wisdom, understanding and knowledge produce an insight into the truths of faith, a discernment that often reaches a clarity and precision astonishing in laypeople strangers to theology. We may recall the praise given by St Jerome to laypeople when Arianism was prevalent. It was their unshakable, uncompromising stand on the Nicene Creed that put to shame theologians and even bishops, who showed themselves confused and faltering. And today, in some places, the bishops are so hindered in their action by unjust restrictions on their liberty that virtually the laity alone can witness to the truth and hand it on to the next generation. Pius XII, in his encyclical *Munificentissimus Deus,* strongly emphasized the theological importance of the people's witness and insight into the faith and, at the same time, stressed the directing and controlling function of the teaching Church.

This sense which the people have for the faith must not be emancipated from the teaching function of the Church. The latter takes into account the sense of the faithful and their witness as a datum of Tradition, which has to be assessed by the teaching authority alone. Cardinal Newman set out clearly the relationship of the teaching authority to the witness of the faithful. He has been reproached for holding that the bishops must "consult" the laity in preparing a doctrinal decision. It would follow, say his critics, that the bishops must take the views of the faithful as their norm in such decisions. Newman answered that the word "consult" in English had no such meaning, that it indicated confidence and esteem rather than subordination; it was a request for information, not an invitation to pronounce judgment. In this sense, we speak of consulting the barometer to find out the existing state of the atmosphere; and similarly the bishops should "consult" the faithful.[5]

Thus the bishops are the primary and official guardians of the Christian revelation, and that is why the early Councils, in their doctrinal decisions, appealed to Scripture and to the tradition of Doctors of the Church and the Fathers who were bishops. But great importance attaches also to the witness of the faithful in general. It constitutes secondary evidence for the Church's tradition; and so, in later times, doctrinal decisions have often taken into account the witness of the faithful and regarded it as a sign of genuine tradition. In a Council the bishops testify to the belief of the Church, without in any way lessening the independence and authority of the teaching body. They do not represent their people in the way a Parliament represents the country. It is their episcopal office, not appointment by the faithful, that makes them at the Council *testes fidei*, witnesses to the faith of the Church. Bishops alone are

[5]Newman *On Consulting the Faithful in Matters of Doctrine* (new edition, London 1961). Erroneous opinions, harking back to the conciliar theories of the late Middle Ages, were put forward at the time of the Vatican Council by the "Old Catholics", Döllinger, Schulte and Friedrich, who wanted to make the bishops representatives of their people rather as members of Parliament are. These views were countered by the Protestant authority on canon law, Hinschius, who showed that, by the tradition of the Councils, the "main ground for holding Councils was the judicial vocation of the Council and of the assembled bishops". See Granderath, I, 86-89. Granderath rightly says that the bishops must "study to acquire the knowledge necessary for their teaching office. For this they have Scripture and Tradition. *One* way to learn the doctrine transmitted by the apostles is certainly to examine what is believed in the whole Church; for it is a Catholic dogma that the whole Church cannot err in matters of faith. Once it is proved that a doctrine is held as of faith by the whole Church, it is thereby proved to be a doctrine of faith. For that reason, Councils, in seeking what is revealed as true, ask what it is that the Church believes. But this is not the only way for the communication of revealed truth . . ." (*ibid.*, p. 90).

the authentic *doctores fidei,* teachers of the faith. When assembled in Council, they represent, in their union with the pope, the whole Church in the most solemn form. But the function of theirs which is mainly stressed by a Council is that of *judices fidei,* judges in matters of faith; it is they who decide questions of doctrine, of Christian life and morals, and their decisions are universally binding. That is the reason why, even in the early Church, it was insisted : *Concilia esse episcoporum* —Councils are the concern of the bishops.[6]

2. Reform of morals

A Council is ecumenical in its execution, when all the bishops have been invited, and have accepted in sufficient numbers to be considered representative of the whole Church. In exceptional circumstances, a minority may be representative. No fixed proportion can be assigned; nor is there any definite rule that can be mechanically applied to determine ecumenicity. In the case of the first eight Councils, only the metropolitans were directly invited, and were commissioned to bring with them some of their suffragans. The important thing was held to be

[6] J. Salaverri, "De Ecclesia Christi", in *Sacrae Theologiae Summa,* 2nd edition, Madrid 1952, pp. 667-668: "The theological foundation of Ecumenical Councils is the divine institution of the apostolic college. For Christ instituted it as a *Corpus capitatum,* consisting of Peter as head and the apostles as members, in order to continue his work on earth with full authority. The apostles under Peter exercised their office either in ordinary fashion, when dispersed, or in extraordinary fashion, when meeting together, as in the Council of Jerusalem (Acts, 15: 6-35). The legal status or authority of Ecumenical Councils rests on the formal apostolic succession; for the episcopal college is formally a continuation of the apostolic college, and so is also a *Corpus capitatum,* consisting of the pope, the successor of St Peter, as head, and the bishops, the successors of the apostles, as members. The bishops under the pope exercise their office, either in ordinary fashion, when dispersed in various parts of the world, or in extraordinary fashion, when assembled in a Council. Thus there is a twofold element of divine institution in the episcopal college, and consequently in Councils. The first is the head, the successor of Peter in the primacy; the second the *Corpus,* the bishops as successors of the apostles . . ."
It would be possible also to explain the representation of the people at Councils by their bishops on the principle: *Episcopus personam gerit Ecclesiae.* This terminology, which is supported by the usage of St Thomas Aquinas, does not affirm any delegation of authority by those who are thus "personified". See Hamer, O.P., in *Lumière et vie, loc. cit.,* pp. 58-59.

the presence of all the patriarchs; but, in many cases, the western patriarchate was represented solely by the papal legates.

With the Councils of Ephesus (431) and Chalcedon (451), the interval between summons and first sitting was too short for all the western bishops to be invited. At the first eight Councils only a few from the west were present; at some only bishops from the east. These Councils, however, were all ecumenical, because the bishop of Rome, as head of the universal Church and, in a special manner, of the west, co-operated with them, as was especially apparent at Ephesus and Chalcedon. It is clear, then, that, in the view of the early Church, the decisive factor was not so much the proportion of bishops present to the whole episcopate as their organic union with their head and centre of unity.

We must distinguish what is strictly necessary for ecumenicity from those factors which make a Council ecumenical in the fullest possible sense. Such factors are :

1. The presence of the bishops in great number, indeed of a majority of them, making the representation of the whole teaching body something real and not merely juridical. This will also ensure a complete presentation of the faith on the part of the teaching body, for the function of witnessing to the faith is inseparable from the episcopal order. Likewise, the bishops' testimony to the beliefs of their subjects can then most fully be presented to the Council.

2. Another factor is free and close discussion of all objections and difficulties. Examples of this are the detailed discussions of the Council of Ferrara (Florence) on the eastern controversies, and those of Trent, lasting more than six months, on the doctrine of justification.

3. Unanimity in their decisions is most desirable; but obviously this is not necessary. A simple majority is sufficient for a valid decision.

To require the actual presence of a majority of bishops would be to overlook the triple function of bishops in a Council. They are not only witnesses and authentic teachers of the faith, but, above all, judges, *judices fidei*. The acts of a Council are essentially judicial, deciding between truth and falsehood, accepting or rejecting a given formula.

Provided that, under the existing conditions, a number of bishops sufficient to represent the whole Church is lawfully assembled, that body acts for all the other members who were invited, though not present. Their resolutions may be rightly said to embody the consensus of the Church as a whole.[7]

3. What makes the decisions ecumenical?

The third kind of ecumenicity, that of authority universally acknowledged, is of greatest importance. It results, as a rule, from the ecumenical summons and the ecumenical assembly; and it is absolutely essential. In case of necessity, it may act as a substitute for the two others, but nothing can ever replace it. The first and second Councils of Constantinople (381 and 553) were neither of them ecumenical in their summons or their actual sitting, since the easterns only were invited and were present; but they became ecumenical through ratification by the pope and the resulting acceptance by the whole Church.

A Council only possesses ecumenical authority if it is the authorized organ of the whole Church. This it cannot be apart from the participation of the pope, for without him the assembled teaching body would lack its visible head and organic centre of unity. That is the reason why the definition of the papal primacy by the Vatican Council has not in any way altered the authority of Councils. There has never been a juridically ecumenical Council without the pope, though his collaboration has taken various forms. The Council of

---

[7] Th. Granderath, *op. cit.*, Vol. I, pp. 88-90.

Chalcedon (451) is a very clear example of the co-operation of bishops with the pope.

In the Church of the first millennium it was a universally accepted principle that no decision in matters of faith could be final and binding on all without the consent of the bishop of Rome.

The decisive authority of Councils rests on the infallibility of their decisions. The theological basis of this is that the episcopal body in union with the Pope is the successor of the Apostolic College. Admittedly, the bishops cannot introduce new revealed truths, as the apostles did, but they possess, as a body, the infallibility Christ promised his Church. When assembled in Council in accord with their visible head, they are kept from error by the assistance of the Holy Spirit. The Church of the living God is called by St Paul "the pillar and ground of truth" (1 Tim. 3 : 15). The bishops as successors of the apostles exercise their teaching function in the most solemn manner when assembled at a Council, and all believers are bound to accept their decisions in matters of faith. For that reason, the early Church held the conviction that ecumenical Councils were infallible. St Ambrose (330-397) affirmed that neither death nor the sword could cut him off from the Council of Nicea.[8] St Augustine (354-430) compares the authority of Councils with that of the apostles,[9] and St Gregory the Great (540-604) goes so far as to say : "I confess that I accept and reverence the four Councils as I do the four Gospels . . ., for they are founded on universal consent".[10] The conviction of the infallibility of Councils was universal till the Reformation, and hardly questioned even at the time of the medieval conciliar movement.

---

[8]M. J. Rouët de Journel, S.J., *Enchiridion Patristicum*, 17th edition, no. 1250.
[9]*Ibid.*, no. 1419, 1535.
[10]*Ibid.*, no. 2291. Cf. H. Bacht, S.J., "Sind die Lehrentscheidungen der ökumenischen Konzilien göttlich inspiriert", in: *Catholica*, 1959, pp. 128-9.

4. The assistance of the Holy Spirit

One of the most current objections to the infallibility of Councils is expressed in the saying that Councils cannot place the Holy Ghost "at their disposal". This popular objection would have been impossible in the time of the ancient Church; it has its origin in an ecclesiology quite other than that of the primitive Church, and bears too the imprint of rationalism.

What is meant by the expression? "Having God at one's disposal" is found only in magical practices and in degenerate forms of religion. The idea is wholly alien to the Christian revelation. In the Council of the Apostles (Acts 15 : 1-35), there is no question of their "having the Holy Ghost at their disposal"; yet they do begin their resolutions with the words: "It has seemed good to the Holy Ghost and to us". The apostles received the revelations of the Holy Ghost, but did not have him at their beck and call. The bishops assembled in Council receive, as we have said, no revelation, they are simply preserved from error in their doctrinal decisions by the Holy Ghost. If we must speak of "disposing", it is rather the bishops who are at the disposal of the Holy Ghost. Yet that would be inexact, for the action of the bishops requires, as a rule, a considerable effort of their own intellects, enlightened by faith. They have to study the questions, search into Scripture and the apostolic tradition, abide by revelation as conveyed in the Old and New Testaments and the doctrinal tradition, and then form their judgment according to conscience and in the presence of Christ, their supreme Lord.

In some Councils, this intellectual activity occasioned such bitterness that the divine assistance was, for some time, indiscernible to the human eye. We have only to think of the violent controversies during the first Councils or of the invasion by iconoclastic soldiers of the Seventh Council, whose first session was forcibly interrupted, so that it had to be transferred from Constantinople to Nicea.

At Trent, Bishop Sanfelice of La Cava, in a quarrel over justification, tore out part of Bishop Dionysius Zanettino's beard, and was expelled from the Council. Besides such eruptions of oriental and southern temperaments, which at any rate are signs of a praiseworthy love of truth, we have the unedifying disputes at the Vatican Council; they indeed attest freedom of speech, but also the presence of an only too human element, from which no Council is wholly free. To argue from these against the assistance of the Holy Ghost in the actual decisions of a Council would be extremely naïve.

The Christian people has always trusted in the assistance of the Holy Ghost at General Councils. It has kept that confidence because it has learned to distinguish human striving and human weakness from the working of God, which is the more marked the more it is countered by human blindness and infirmity. We see exemplified in Councils what St Paul says is the feature of Christ's whole redemptive action—"Power is made perfect in infirmity" (2 Cor. 12 : 9). At the moment when he stresses the splendour of the apostolic office, he confesses : "But we have this treasure in earthen vessels, that the excellency may be of the power of God, and not of us" (2 Cor. 4 : 7). In God's hands, the tool's defects do not prevent a successful outcome, but make it all the more wonderful, and point all the more clearly to the real cause. The infallible teaching office is entrusted to human weakness; and all can see that it is not human wisdom and theological learning, nor yet high sanctity and a faith that can move mountains, but the assistance of the Holy Spirit that guarantees the infallibility of Councils, preserving its members from error.

It would, therefore, be both unrealistic and unchristian to argue from the shortcomings of the members to the falsity of their teaching. It is no matter for surprise that the participants in a Council should be found to share the weaknesses of their contemporaries. Yet the unbiased historian must admit that the members of Councils come out well from such a comparison, and, in fact, rise consistently above the prejudices and passions of their time. In the Church, so widely spread over the world, justice and truth naturally encounter obstacles, and these may be found too within Councils themselves. But it remains true that, both in the Church at large and in Councils, the redemptive work of Christ, through the activity of the Spirit, continues to preserve revealed truth and to keep the Church's official and universal teaching from error.

The bishops gathered in a Council are far from imagining they have the Holy Spirit at their disposition. On the contrary, they are well aware that their own ability, their theological learning and subtlety, are inadequate to the magnitude of the work at hand. For that reason, the Council opens with prayer to the Holy Spirit; in fact, its session is not only an act of jurisdiction, or of the teaching and pastoral office, but a liturgical celebration.[11] The liturgical part is not just an appendage or a decorative feature, but belongs to the essence of the Council, which, in fulfilling its function, performs an act of divine worship. In the Roman Ceremonial, the meeting of the Council begins with a Mass of the Holy Ghost, in whose action all their hopes are placed. There too is the basis of the great expectations the ordinary Christian has of the Council; for the Spirit of God can do what is impossible by human reckoning. He knows ways and means to the unity of Christians, which are hidden from us. In that hope, all who believe in Christ as the Son of God and redeemer of the world can join in the prayer: Thou who has gathered people of all tongues to unity of faith, send forth thy Spirit, and all things will be renewed.

---

[11] Cf. *Collectio Lacensis*, Vol. vii, *op. cit.*, col. 694-699. C. Butler, *The Vatican Council*, p. 131: "The general Congregations always began with a Low Mass of the Holy Ghost, celebrated by an Archbishop."

V

The Forthcoming Council as a Manifestation of the Unity and Catholicity of the Church

On 25th January, 1959, at the conclusion of the world octave of prayer for unity, Pope John XXIII announced the second Vatican Council, which should also be an invitation to our separated brethren to seek unity. In an address on 9th August, 1959, the Pope expressly stated that it was when he was meditating, in the unity octave, on Christ's sacerdotal prayer and his prayer for unity that the idea of a Council came "like the spontaneous flowering of an unexpected spring", not as the fruit of long consideration, but—as the Pope said elsewhere—as a sudden inspiration from above, a personal intimation by the Holy Spirit.

1. What subjects will the Council consider?

It is still too early to do more than guess at individual subjects; but we may point out that the Councils of Trent and of the Vatican both remained incomplete. The former dealt with the doctrine on Scripture and Tradition, original sin and justification, and on the sacraments, but not with that of the Church itself, though this was the focal point of the disputes between Protestants and Catholics. The split between the two sides was fundamentally over the doctrine of the Church. But the Council was constantly under pressure of time and the conclusion of its final period was rushed through too hastily, owing to the pope's serious illness and the likelihood of his death.

Three hundred years later, the Vatican Council intended to

bring out the doctrine "on the Church of Christ" omitted by Trent. The outline submitted to the Fathers on 21st January, 1870, and expanded on 6th March, dealt with the Church and its structure in fifteen chapters.[12] Only the two on papal primacy and infallibility could be discussed and officially decided dogmatically. The rest were left, because the outbreak of the Franco-Prussian war and the siege of Rome by the Piedmontese army forced the prorogation of the Council. Before the discussion on the primacy and infallibility, a decree was issued, in the third session on 24th April, 1870, "on the Catholic Faith", in which the errors of the time, agnosticism, pantheism and so-called "Hermesianism" were condemned, and which dealt, in four chapters, with the existence and our knowledge of a personal God, the necessity of divine revelation, the nature of faith, and the relation between faith and natural knowledge.[13]

After a lapse of ninety years, it is hardly possible to summon a Council that would be simply a continuation of the former. For that reason, as Cardinal Tardini explained in his address on 31st October, 1959, the coming Council will be called the Second Vatican Council, and, like the first, hold its sessions in the Basilica of St Peter.[14]

In his concluding address to the Roman diocesan synod, Pope John declared: "Oecumenicum Concilium convocandum ... Vaticanum secundum vocabitur". He placed the Council under the protection of the "Patriarchs of Constantinople, Gregory of Nazianzen and John Chrysostom, and of Pope Gregory the Great".

Cardinal Montini, the archbishop of Milan, pointed out in the speech already alluded to that the coming Second Vatican Council would be the first in history that had neither to

---

[12]*Collectio Lacensis*, Vol. VII, *op. cit.* col. 567-578; col. 641.
[13]Denz. 1781-1820.
[14]*Osservatore Romano*, 1st November, 1959.

surmount internal discord nor to solve problems of doctrine disputed within the Church. On the contrary, the Church was to take cognizance of what was demanded by her growing life, of her evangelizing mission and of her own spiritual needs. Among other duties of the Council, he mentioned that of completing the doctrine of episcopal authority, considering the relations between the religious orders and the bishops, and the necessity of greater participation of the laity in the life of the Church. But the two greatest problems were, undoubtedly, the union of all Christians, which admittedly could not be attained all at once, and how to counter the moral crisis the world was experiencing in such tragic contrast to its technical progress. The Fathers of the Council, he went on, would not fail in authoritative declarations against the ideological errors of the present time.

The aims and themes of the coming Council have been repeatedly stated by the Pope to be the strengthening of faith, moral renewal, the adaptation of ecclesiastical legislation to changed conditions, and the preparation of a future reunion of those outside the Church. These may well be called extremely general aims, and one Protestant dignitary has spoken regretfully of the "insubstantiality" of the statements made about the Council up to the present. But if we look closely, we can see there is a single basic idea running through all that the Pope has said on the most various occasions. It is his favourite idea, to which he always returns, and which he designates as the actual programme of the Council. The *leitmotive* of all the discussions of the Council is to be the manifestation of the one, holy, catholic and apostolic Church in her Unity and Catholicity. The two great encyclicals of John XXIII, *Ad Petri Cathedram* (29th June, 1959) and *Princeps Pastorum* (28th November, 1959) clarify both the unity and the catholicity of the Church, and the two documents lay down in advance the basic programme of the Council.

Great as are the possibilities of a successful outcome, we must not ignore the difficulties in the way of the Council arising from the changed conditions of the present time. Doubtless, the Church stands in her catholic unity as a sign raised aloft among the nations, and she stands in no danger within from heresy or schism. It is also true that there is not the same need of reform as there was at the time of the Council of Trent, and that the administration of the Church works very smoothly. What, then, is the reason for a Council? All Councils have a twofold aspect, one doctrinal, the other disciplinary; and one or the other of these predominates according to the exigencies of the time. It would seem that, in the coming Council, questions concerning the practical application of Christianity will be foremost, and that they will be considered in the light of determined theological principles. In his first encyclical, *Ad Petri cathedram*, Pope John enumerated the chief objects of the Council as the development of the Catholic faith, the moral renovation of Christian life, and the adjustment of ecclesiastical discipline to the needs and methods of the present. Consequently, a good part of its work will be to find the right answers to those problems which have arisen through the changes in the world since the time of the Vatican Council.

2. *Present conditions call for a new exposition of the catholicity of the Church*

Councils always mark important turning-points in the Church's history; and we are now at one of them. The Church is obliged to take account of the wholly altered state of the world, if it is to fulfil its mission. This new situation is due to three great revolutions :

a. The relations between State and Church.—The Emperor Constantine was the first ruler to take the Church under his protection, so beginning a new era in Christian history. It was

99

the start of the golden age, in which all members of the State were Christians, and Church and State grew up alongside to form a *Civitas Christiana*. Ideally at least, emperor and kings strove to bring about St Augustine's City of God. The union of Church and State underwent its first shock with the rise of nation-states in Europe in the sixteenth century, and it ended with the secularization of the State in the eighteenth.[15] Today the Constantinian relation between Church and State is exceptional, even in Christian countries. There are few governments that actively support the Church and work in harmony with her. The change arose partly through the secularization of modern culture and partly through a stronger sense of the Church's autonomy. Instead of the former close harmony, we see a friendly attitude, indeed, on the part of many governments, a neutral one with others, and overt hostility on the part of quite a few. In Communist countries, Christianity and Church are looked on as survivals of a bygone age, and themselves about to disappear.

b. *The right of supremacy of a world-wide Christian culture is being called in question.*—At the time of the Vatican Council, and even till the outbreak of the first world-war, the dominant European and American culture was still based on Christian principles. Its ethical foundations were not simply an echo of the Gospel and the moral teaching of the Church, but were the outcome too of the contact of Christianity with the social, political, economic and cultural elements of European and American history. The peoples of Asia and Africa held in

---

[15]There is much talk nowadays about the end of the "Constantine epoch", which expression means that from the time of Constantine to about the French Revolution, Church and State worked in close association in many departments of life. The contributors to Herders *Bildungsbuch*, Freiburg, 1953, p. 351, use the expression in a broader sense, which is becoming more and more widely adopted. Strictly speaking, the "Constantine epoch" should be restricted to the East Roman Empire, and roughly to the time up to the beginning of the seventh century or perhaps to the foundation of the Western Empire in 800.

admiration the advanced civilization of the west and Europe's spiritual culture with its ethical roots. This world-wide regard for "Christian culture" created a favourable prospect for the work of the missions.

The situation is now dramatically altered. The two wars have destroyed the prestige of western culture in the eyes of the coloured races. At the same time, a large part of the traditionally Christian white peoples has fallen under Communist domination; and their governments work to replace Christianity by Marxism. We see how, not so far away, an attempt is being made to replace the Christian meaning of Christmas by an antichristian ideology. Even in many democratic countries of the free world a secularized culture prevails, indifferent or inimical to Christianity. The result is that, there too, the Church is conscious of being in the minority, and that its influence on public life is waning.[16]

c. *The colonial epoch is over.*—The colonial period began with the discovery of America in the fifteenth century, and lasted four hundred and fifty years, till the end of the second world war. It saw a world-wide expansion of European power, industry and culture. Missionaries had no other aim than preaching the Gospel, but they were helped in this by the enormous prestige of the Christian countries with the coloured peoples. On this account, they became, whether they wanted to or not, a means for communicating their own native culture. But it was no fault of theirs that their work of evangelization became linked with the expansion of European spheres of influence. Up to the first world war, the favourable prospects of the missions in Asia and Africa were practically unlimited. The superiority of the Christian culture and of the civilization of Europe and America was unquestioned; and the ineffective

---

[16]Cf. A. Rademacher, *Kultur*, in: *LThK*, Vol. VI, pp. 291-4, on the Church's basic attitude to culture.

pagan nature-religions were no longer considered serious rivals of Christianity.

Today nearly all the colonial regimes have disappeared. In spite of much injustice, they had favoured, in one way or another, the spread of western Christian culture and the work of the missions. They have been replaced by nationalistic governments, often suspicious and unfriendly, even directly hostile, to Christianity. Furthermore, the world-wide, techno-logical civilization of the present day is wholly secular. Fifty years ago, mankind in general still lived, in some degree, under the influence of a culture whose roots were Christian; but now the majority is subject either to the Communist ideology or to the influence of revived non-Christian natural-religions. Bud-dhism, Hinduism and Mohammedanism have awakened to new life and self-awareness and seek to develop a modern culture corresponding to their own religious outlook. Allied to their revival is an ardent nationalism, which sees Christianity as a hostile religion.[17]

If we in the west want to help the peoples of Asia and Africa to solve their own problems, we have to apply ourselves to understanding their spiritual and religious traditions. "Cer-tainly many misunderstandings will have to be overcome. But the more we pay attention to what these other religions have to say to us, the clearer we will perceive the tremendous unease that lies at their heart. There was in them a longing which can find fulfilment only in him who is the way, the truth, and the life, namely Christ" (G. Schückler).

Fifty years ago, it looked as if the course of history was almost inevitably bringing about the spread of the kingdom of God over the earth; but the situation has changed completely. The course of history now seems to oppose the Church's mission. The great "Soviet Encyclopaedia", published in 1958, foretells,

---

[17]Cf. W. A. Visser't Hooft, "Importance of the Asian Churches in the ecumenical movement", in: *Eglise Vivante*, Vol. XI, 1959, pp. 420-433.

in the article on missions, a complete breakdown of missionary work. In view of the increasing obstacles, Christians themselves may be tempted to despair.

But God's Word remains unfettered. The great mistake of the enemies of Christianity is to judge the Church by political and sociological standards. No doubt, the history of the Church as a visible society is affected by political and social factors, but as founded by Christ and led by the Spirit it has its own proper laws of development and is not to be explained solely by natural causes.

3. The new state of the world needs the Catholicity of the Church

In his encyclical *Princeps Pastorum,* Pope John XXIII, looking confidently into the future, foreshadows the ways of adapting the missions to the changed situation. What he is concerned with is the unfolding of the full catholicity of the Church, which is open to all peoples and races, all cultures and civilizations, all genuine ethical and religious values. This unfolding is governed by four principles :

1. The Church is not to be identified with any particular culture or civilization, not even that of the west.

2. The Roman and Greek culture of the Mediterranean peoples was, indeed, determined by Providence as the cradle of Christianity in its infancy. "In regard to many unessential matters of ritual, organization, art and science, the present outlook of the Church would be very different if it had its origin in China, for example, instead of the Hellenistic world."[18]

3. As the Church purified Hellenistic culture, retaining and vivifying all its goodness and excellence, so she will clear away all the errors intermingled with the real values of other religions and cultures, elevating and transfiguring them. All that is good, true and noble in the religions and cultures of the world comes

---

[18]S. Tromp, S.J., *De Revelatione Christiana,* Rome, 1950.

from God, the source of all the excellencies manifested in his creatures.

4. Although the Church's faith and essential structure are of divine origin and have been determined by Christ for all time, Christ's message, though one and unchanging, is received variously according to the character of peoples and their cultures, and takes on visible form in religious practices and ritual. God's revelation is profound and comprehensive, and peoples of different cultures feel a special affinity to one or other aspect corresponding to their own individuality.[19]

The Church's catholicity means that she possesses the fullness of truth, which is always capable of being expressed in more perfect fashion up to the end of time. The Church is in continual growth, and, without sullying the purity of God's word, takes to herself new values, cultures and forms of life, and gives them a fresh splendour.

This is what Gertrude von le Fort means when she makes the Church say :

"I was secretly in the temples of their gods;
I was dimly in the utterances of all their sages;
I was there on the towers of their star-gazers;
I was the longing of all ages;
I was the light of all times, I am the fullness of all times;
In me all come together, in me all are eternally one;
I am the way of all ways; along me march on to God the millennia".

The Church proclaims the Gospel for every age, every people, every civilization, as she did in the heroic age of the first three centuries before Constantine. That does not imply a repetition of the early history of the Church. She is organic, and her existing state cannot be replaced by that of the pre-Con-

[19]Cf. H. Dumoulin, S.J., "Gedanken zur religiösen Begegnung von Ost und West" in: *Stimmen der Zeit*, Vo. 165, 1959-60, pp. 265-274; R. André, "L'Eglise à l'heure de Jean XXIII" in *La Revue nouvelle*, Vol. XXX, 1959, pp. 498-513.

stantine age, any more than a tree can be cut back to its roots and first beginnings. The Church has her own laws of growth, and one of them concerns her adaptability to new conditions. She lives in a kind of symbiosis with the world. While preserving the faith given her once and for all by God and the basic structure established by Christ, she must continue to adjust herself to her changing environment. So it is that her outward appearance and her pastoral methods were different in the early Christian age, the high Middle Ages, the post-Tridentine period, and the nineteenth century. And the future Council will see a notable advance in her adaptation to the present time and to the world of the future.

The Church is neither national nor international, but simply catholic and universal. No country can look on her as something alien; she belongs to all nations and peoples, quite irrespective of race or colour. Everywhere she has right of citizenship, wherever there are human beings and communities; for all men are called to be sons of God, and the Church of God is the common mother of all.

These are the principles governing missionary work, which aims at establishing in every country a normal hierarchy of native bishops. The number and quality of the native clergy is the true criterion of missionary work in any district.[20]

4. The Church's mission in the world today

The problems of the Church's apostolate in the changed world must be given an important place. As we have seen, all the Councils gave prominence to questions of the relation of the Church to the world. In the Middle Ages, questions about "Christendom", that comprehensive and ordered structure, often took the first place in the programme of Councils. In the Councils of Trent and the Vatican the activity of the Church

---

[20]R. Musaragno, "La Chiesa nei territori di Missione", in: *Osservatore Romano*, 17th April, 1960.

in the world had its place in the programme, but considered in a new fashion suited to the changed circumstances; this was the case both with the chapters on dogma—we have only to think of the Vatican decisions on the relations between faith and reason—and more particularly with the decrees concerning reform.

The pastoral letter of the Italian bishops to the clergy, of 25th March, 1960, puts in the forefront the question of the relations of the Church to the world. It bases this relationship on the Incarnation : the incarnate Son of God has set all human problems in their true light, laid down the principles to be applied, and provided the means for their solution. In modern times there has arisen a form of humanism which aims at solving all problems by purely natural and human means, and deliberately ignores, or openly opposes, the Incarnation and all that follows from it. It fails to see that, if men deny and set aside supernatural revelation, they cannot even give an account of nature in its totality, and sink below the human level, which is that of a spiritual nature ordained to God.

The Italian bishops ask whether there lies at the root of all modern false ideologies and wrongful practices in the religious and moral sphere a single basic error from which all the others arise. They reply that there does, that it consists in a "tendency, or more exactly a mentality, which rejects, systematically and emphatically, any influence of religion in general and the Catholic hierarchy in particular on human life and institutions. We are confronted with a purely natural conception of life, in which the pronouncements of religion are either expressly rejected or confined to the secret domain of conscience and the mystic twilight of the Church, without any sort of right to interfere in or influence public life, whether in the philosophical, legal, industrial, artistic, scientific, social or political spheres."[21]

[21]*Osservatore Romano*, 15th April, 1960.

106

The doctrinal error of naturalism and false humanism makes its appearance in two distinct forms :

1. Materialistic atheism attacks every kind of belief in God as an "ideology" from a past age, and to be superseded. The brute force of organized atheism is something repulsive to anyone with any kind of religion.

2. Another form is modern "laicism", which acknowledges God and religion, but rejects the supernatural order arising from the Incarnation, denying that it is a living and dynamic force in history. "In building the *civitas terrena* it wholly ignores the prescriptions of the Christian revelation and disputes the Church's claim to a mission to act, on spiritual grounds, in the temporal order, by directing, informing and stimulating its activities".[22] On this view, the Christian faith is an exclusively private concern, and, as regards public life, the only relevant factors are man's natural endowments, disconnected utterly from any relation to a supernatural order of truth and morality. The believer is, therefore, free to confess his faith in his private life, but he may not try to shape the life of the community according to the teachings of the Gospel. The Church is admitted to possess independent and sovereign power to exercise its specifically religious activities for a directly supernatural end (for example, in matters of worship, the administration of the sacraments, and preaching), but has no right whatever to intervene in public life, which, in virtue of its complete juridical and moral autonomy, can admit no dependence on, or even prompting by, "external religious doctrines".

These opinions are clearly contrary to Catholic teaching. "In practice they deny or ignore the historical fact of revelation, misconceive the nature and mission of the Church, and tend to break up the unity of the Christian life, which knows no cleavage between private and public life. They hand over the decision between truth and falsehood, good and evil, to the

[22] *ibid.*

107

arbitrary choice of the individual or the collectivity, and open the door to all kinds of individual and social errors, of which recent decades provide so many frightful instances".[23]

All this raises and accentuates the problem of the Freedom of the Church. How can the Church in the modern world exercise her mission in its entire scope? Militant atheism, based on a materialistic ideology and embodied in an organized society, aims at eliminating all belief in God, and tolerates the Church's activities only for the time being in the sanctuary and in private life. There is, too, a vague kind of deism, which separates God wholly from the world, and admits a naturalistic humanism as the sole standard in the things of the world; consequently, it also opposes the Church's activity in what belongs to social ethics and the life of the community. But the State is not superior to the moral law, nor is it the source of ethical principles. Unless the State acknowledges God, it makes itself God, and so becomes totalitarian, self-divinized, and imposing its own philosophy of life, which leaves no possible scope for the unfettered activity of the Church.

Opposition to the influence of the Christian Church seemed, in the immediate post-war years, to have largely disappeared. The war had shattered all the certainties of life, the totalitarian ideologies had let loose a deluge of barbarism, and the Church seemed to many outside observers the only defence of human freedom and dignity, the guardian of all spiritual values. But now that the storm has subsided in many countries and life is once again normal, men forget the menace constantly overhanging them, and want to restrain the Church from "invading" the spheres of culture and the life of the community.

In the non-catholic world, too, particular attention has been given to the problems of the relation of the Christian message

---

[23]ibid. Cf. F. Kempf, S.J., "Die Katholische Lehre von der Gewalt der Kirche über das Zeitliche in ihrer geschichtlichen Entwicklung seit dem Investiturstreit," in: *Catholica*, Vol. XII (1958), pp. 50-66.

to the world and its institutions. In spite of their differing
theological positions—we may recall the differing conception
on "Law and Gospel" in the Lutheran and reformed theology[24]
—all the Protestant Confessions and the Church of England
have studied afresh the problem of the relation of the Church
and the Gospel to the cultural, social and political environment. The ecumenical movement held that one of its principal
functions was to create a hearing for the "voice of the Christian
conscience in the world" and to further social justice and
peace. The "Ecumenical Movement for Practical Christianity", founded at the first world-conference in Stockholm in
1925, has been continued, since 1938, in the "World Council
for Practical Christianity". The second world-conference at
Oxford was faced with the problem of defending the freedom
of the Christian conscience against the totalitarian State. The
reports from Amsterdam and Evanston show the attitude
taken, from the Gospel standpoint, to concrete questions of the
day concerning Christianity. The "Commission of the Churches
for international affairs" is the organ of the World Council of
Churches and the World Council for Missions in the creation
of international order based on justice.

At the first plenary assembly of the World Council of
Churches in Amsterdam, 1948, the idea of the "responsible
society" was taken to express the aim of Christian thought and
action in society. "A responsible society is one where freedom
means the freedom of men who realize their responsibility for
justice and the ordering of public life, and where those who
hold political authority or economic power are responsible for
its exercise to God and to men whose well-being depends on
it . . .

"Therefore we oppose :
(a) all attempts to restrict the freedom of the Church to bear
witness to the Lord and his scheme of salvation, and every

[24]Cf. P. Bläser, "Gesetz und Evangelium" in: *Catholica* 14, (1960), pp. 1-23.

attempt at prejudicing freedom to obey God and to act according to conscience; these freedoms are bound up with man's responsibility before God;

(b) any denial of the right to share in the shaping of society, for this is a duty bound up with man's responsibility towards his neighbour;

(c) any attempt at obstructing men in investigating and spreading the truth."[25]

The second plenary assembly in Evanston, 1954, dealt with the "responsible society in relation to the modern planned State and to the problems of the underdeveloped countries", and concluded that "the responsible society is not just an alternative social or political system, but a criterion by which all existing social systems are to be assessed, and, at the same time, a guide directing us in the decisions we have to take from time to time. Christians are called to live responsibly, that is, according to the demands of God's redemptive action in Christ, in whatever kind of social order, even the most unfavourable".[26]

A number of Protestant theologians wanted a thorough study of the scriptural and theological bases of the concepts of "responsible society", justice and ethical freedom. This raised the burning question of the nature of the authority of Scripture in every sphere of life, and there was a clear division on exegetical principles between the different Confessions and theological schools.[27] The questions of the Church's nature and unity remain unsolved problems in the background of the discussions within the ecumenical movement.

The Italian bishops' pastoral letter in its main enunciations is of great importance for the whole Christian world. The

---

[25]P. Abrecht, "Verantwortliche Gesellschaft", in: *Weltkirchenlexicon*, Stuttgart, 1959, col. 1528-9.
[26]*ibid.*
[27]Heinz Horst Schrey, "Weltbild und Weltanschauung", in: *Weltkirchenlexicon, op. cit.*, col. 1578.

problem it treats of will necessarily be envisaged by the Council in its efforts to revitalize Christian life. In these times there are current any number of grave errors menacing the Christian life. They are all the more dangerous in that they are not just philosophies, but betray the presence of a definite feeling about human life and settled way of living. No doubt, these current misconceptions will be countered by the Council by a clear exposition of the great Christian principles of God's sovereignty over the whole creation, of the Incarnation, the authority of the Church, and the Christian idea of man. Admittedly, at the present preliminary stage, this is only a supposition, as is also the desire that has been expressed that the Council should, in a solemn pronouncement, bring home the Christian view of the world and human life to burdened and anguished humanity.[28]

In ultimate analysis, all the errors of the present run counter to the Christian doctrine on the Church. The Italian pastoral letter shows how atheism, deism, erroneous views of man, disregard of the Incarnation and of Revelation, all result in opposition, both in theory and practice, to the Church in her nature and mission. Error and ignorance about "the mystery of the Church, her rights, her relations both internal and external"[29] are the causes of the secularization of thought and practice which leads to such tragic results. The Italian pastoral urges a thorough study of ecclesiology on the lines of the encyclicals *Mystici corporis* and *Mediator Dei*. "This will carry us beyond the external and legal aspect of the Church to an understanding of the great mystery of her indispensable role of mediator between God and the souls of men, and of the sublime nature of her spiritual mission in human history. It will

---

[28]These ideas have been constantly reiterated by the popes; e.g. Pius XII in his Christmas broadcast of 1942 (*AAS* XXXV, 1943, pp. 16-22), especially the section on the Christian idea of the State, *ibid.*, pp. 21-22.

[29]R. Aubert, "Qu' est-ce qu'un concile?" in *La Revue Nouvelle*, Vol. XXX (1959), p. 488.

show up the enormity of the error of those who think they are working for the kingdom of God, while cutting themselves off from community with the Church and the hierarchy which guides her".[30]

The pastoral letter warns against "opposing the charismatic Church to the hierarchical, and the inward promptings of the heart to the external disciplinary order, through separating the visible forms of Christianity from its profound supernatural essence on the ground that love is sufficient without any kind of juridical ordinances".[31]

It is far from the intention of the bishops' pastoral to diminish the role of the laity in the Church—"at all times lay-people were the Church's strength and pride, and were accorded the lofty functions of a true priesthood under the authoritative guidance of the hierarchy".[32] What the pastoral is concerned with is to set out plainly the distinction between the hierarchical priesthood and the royal priesthood of all believers. It is a fundamental error to promote the "theology of the laity" by minimizing the distinction between the two kinds of priesthood. The lack of co-operation of the laity in the Church's apostolate is not to be ascribed to the existence of a hierarchical priesthood of divine origin which restrains lay action. On the contrary, the Church's hierarchical structure is the strongest incentive for the laity to take part in the apostolate. This has been convincingly demonstrated by recent popes. A further proof is given by what we see in Protestant parishes. If the above allegation were true, the laity in these parishes ought to evince untold activity, for they possess no sort of divinely appointed hierarchy to restrain them. But what is actually the case? Dr Hendrik Kraemer, professor at Leiden,

---

[30]Cf. *Osservatore Romano*, 15th April, 1960, p. 2.
[31]*Ibid.*, p. 4.
[32]Article "Laicismo" in: *Osservatore Romano*, 16th April, 1960. (A commentary on the Pastoral Letter of the Italian Bishops which we have already mentioned, which is intended directly for the clergy.)

Holland and a former director of the Ecumenical Institute in Bossey near Geneva, gives his view in *A Theology of the Laity*. "We had hoped", he writes, "that the Reformers, in getting rid of the hierarchy, had thereby abolished the inferior status of the laity. But it turned out otherwise, and we have only been subjected to another form of clericalism. We have always had, and still have, 'pastor-churches', where everything is regulated by churchmen, and the ordinary members remain passive. We have solved the question of rights in our own way, but we are embarrassed by the actual state of affairs; and, indeed, it is the Catholics who are developing the theology of the laity at present". Kraemer makes no secret of the debt he owes to Catholic writers for his own ideas.[33]

An article on "the priesthood of all believers" in *Osservatore Romano*, 14th April, 1960,[34] discusses the subject in theological detail, and clarifies the pastoral letter in this matter. It reviews the subject in the light of Scriptural exegesis, patristic teaching, liturgy and dogma, as well as of the doctrinal pronouncements of the popes, and rightly insists on the paramount importance of the doctrine of the priesthood of all believers for the sanctification of the people, their participation in the Eucharist, and the Church's apostolate. The pastoral letter warns priests to avoid, in their dealings with the laity, all undue emphasis on their authority, and admonishes them to work with the laity in a spirit of love and respect, to be prudent in moderating rash suggestions, to give every attention to all reasonable proposals, to furnish religious and ethical incentives, and appeal constantly to personal initiative and responsibility.

---

[33]H. Kraemer, *A Theology of the Laity*, London, 1958, p. 192-3.
[34]Pius XI saw the "apostolate of the laity" as beginning in apostolic times. He described "Catholic Action" as "the co-operation of the laity in the hierarchical apostolate of the Church", and frequently insisted that this definition was chosen only after careful consideration and "not without divine prompting". It was based on St Paul's epistle to the Philippians, 4: 3. A number of other passages in St Paul show how laypeople worked under him in spreading the Gospel.

Finally, the bishops warn their clergy "not to interfere in specialized fields where they have no right to give directives since decisions there must be left to the free choice of the individual".

Besides upholding the Christian idea of man and renewing the life of the Church, will the Council pursue the doctrine on the Church left uncompleted by the first Vatican Council, and in that context, deal with the priesthood of the laity? H Jedin,[35] the greatest authority on conciliar history, gives the following opinion. "The principal function of General Council has always been to ensure the teaching of the faith through defining Catholic doctrine against contemporary errors. There have been Councils that have not issued any disciplinar decrees, but none which has not either countered error or excommunicated some heretic. No error of our own time is so momentous as the distortion, the denial, of the Christian idea of man found in atheistic social teaching. No truth of faith in the present 'age of the Church', so urgently needs precise formulation as the nature of the Church itself. But Church history has no prophetical function. It makes no pretence to foist its advice on the responsible leaders of the Church. All it does is to give them, through knowledge of the past, a clearer insight into the present and the future".

We may assume, with some probability, that the doctrine on the Church, left unfinished by the first Vatican Council will be taken up again and completed by the second. For some decades now, it has been said, rightly enough, that the twentieth century will be called "the century of the Church". For the Church has come to occupy the attention of men far more than ever before; and, in addition, it is increasingly the subject of theological works. Research in biblical theology patristic studies, the history of theology, have all thrown fresh

---

[35] *Ecumenical Councils in the Catholic Church, op. cit.*

light on the Church's nature and structure. Theological controversy has made it clear that the doctrine on the Church is the crucial point dividing the Christian confessions. As a result, ways have been sought to overcome the divisions in Christendom, and to reach some sort of unity of the Churches. In the case of Protestants, Anglicans and part of Orthodox Christendom, this longing for unity has found organized expression in the World Council of Churches. It is realized that this Council is far from being the union aimed at or ever will be, but that its function is to seek unremittingly for ways to achieve this. Pope John alluded to this earnest striving after unity in his first encyclical *Ad Petri Cathedram,* and proceeded to expound, from Scripture and Tradition, the doctrine of the unity of the Church as willed by Christ.

Before that, Pius XII had signalized the central importance of the doctrine on the Church in the theological context of this century, and published to the world his encyclical *Mystici Corporis,* which might well form the basis of a comprehensive ecclesiology. In this connection, special attention must be given to the question of the apostolic succession of bishops. It is one closely bound up with the problems of the Church's structure, her teaching authority, tradition and the validity of bishops' and priests' orders, and, in recent years, it has been in the forefront of the theological works even of non-Catholics. The results of recent studies on the theology of St Ignatius of Antioch, St Irenaeus of Lyons and Tertullian are relevant here. In addition, the findings of research into the New Testament and patristic teaching on the Church will have to be assessed. New light will thus be thrown by ecclesiology on the place of the laity in the Church and its responsibility for the kingdom of God, a point on which recent popes have given explicit guidance.

The first Vatican Council had to safeguard the truths of faith from current errors; and today Christianity sees itself menaced even more radically. There has never been a Council which has not had to meet some attack or reject some current error. The history of past Councils makes it likely that the one about to be held will meet the denial of the Christian view of man by atheistic ideology and sociology with a clear definition of the Church's teaching.

VI

The Renewal of Christian Life

The radical change in social conditions, due to the advance of science and the raising of material standards, has given rise to new problems on various levels. There is too an urgent need to uphold the religious and ethical principles of private, family and public life, which many are misguided enough to despise as relics of medievalism or else ignore in practice. In this matter an ecumenical Council can powerfully contribute to a moral revival among the people. That was why, twenty years ago, Cardinal Ruffini, Archbishop of Palermo, urged Pius XII to summon an ecumenical Council, pointing out that it would have as many pressing problems to deal with as the Council of Trent.[36]

The Council of Trent, as is well known, was a reforming Council; and the future Council too will aim at reform and the renewal of Christian life, as Pope John XXIII has often repeated. On 6th April, 1959, he expressed the hope that it would renew the power of the apostolate and prove to the world that the Gospel has strength to reform and elevate mankind. The Council of Trent is a striking and altogether amazing example of a comprehensive reform of the kind. There the

[36] *Osservatore Romano*, 4th November, 1959.

Fathers of the Council did not simply restore medieval Catholicism, but devised laws and pastoral practices suitable to the changed conditions and needs of the time, nor did they shrink from radical measures. Abuses that had crept in were firmly rejected, new forms of administration and pastoral care adopted, and the Church was given a structure enabling it to renew itself and withstand unimpaired all the storms to come.

The Council of Trent was confronted by a changed world; and, likewise, the Council about to take place faces quite new conditions, which require corresponding changes in the law of the Church. At the very beginning of the encyclical *Ad Petri Cathedram,* the Pope speaks of the "adjustment of the Church's law to present needs", and of the "enactment of an up-to-date code of laws for the Church of the eastern rite". He goes on to say that he intends to summon the ecumenical Council so that bishops from all parts may deal with the grave religious questions of the day, promote the growth of the Church and the renewal of the moral life, and adjust Church discipline to the necessities of the time.

Among these problems of adjustment, that of the missions is of particular urgency. The Council will be faced with such a changed world as could scarcely be envisaged at the time of Trent or the Vatican. The salient feature is the desire of the coloured peoples for partnership with the rest on equal terms. At the time of Trent, America had been discovered, and the colonial period had begun. The problems of the age had started to emerge, well described by Reinhold Schneider in his work, *Las Casas before Charles V.* But the present situation is quite different. Europe's vision had indeed been broadened by the discovery of America, but the coloured races remained isolated as they had been for centuries. The initiative in history was still with the people of Europe and the Near East. Asia and Africa were strangers to scientific progress, technology, cultural advance. Nonetheless, the colonial period was preparing the great upheaval of our time. The coloured races have woken up. They have appropriated the results of European science and technology, but unfortunately have often adopted the rationalism, materialism and communistic sociology of the nineteenth century, along with the nationalistic spirit prevailing widely in Europe. Nor are their demands by any means satisfied. As Cardinal Siri, Archbishop of Genoa, in a speech on 18th November, 1959, about the historical functions of the Council, pointed out, a wholly new situation has arisen and must be met.[37]

Pope John XXIII, in his missionary encyclical *Princeps Pastorum* of 1959, has already given his answer to the demands of the present time. He calls for a still more thorough training of the native clergy, a training adapted to their own environment and making use of the special qualities, the civilization and customs of the coloured races; also the training of an educated laity as witnesses to Christ on their own initiative and responsibility in the social-ethical and allied spheres. The papal directives will have great importance for the Council's deliberations on missionary problems and will help to bring out the functions of the laity in general in the Church. The Council will therefore have to take account of the reactions of the coloured people to European colonialism in the missions; and missionary methods will have to be reassessed and studied in the light of the Gospel and the nature of the universal Church. The law of the Church, her methods of evangelization and ecclesiastical usages in the missions, must be brought into line with the changed environment, and this "accommodation" must be carefully thought out. A General Council affords the best possible scope for solving all these problems.

1. The spirit of faith and the problems of a scientific age

As happened four hundred years ago, the coming Council

---

[37] *Osservatore Romano*, 20th November 1959, Cf. R. André, *op. cit.*

will effect a real reform in the Church, an intensified spirit of faith, a fresh flowering of the Christian life, a renewal of pastoral activity, and legislation appropriate to the present situation.

The spirit of darkness tries to turn men's minds from the things of eternity and awareness that they are made in the divine image. It deludes man with the mirage of independence of God so as to enslave him to a soulless collectivism. When the Council of Trent came to an end, the modern era had already begun. Science investigated the laws of nature and made them subservient to man. All sorts of inventions appeared, and the methods of rational inquiry and of the scientific solution of problems were also applied to the spheres of social life, medical care and population problems. Mankind has achieved wonderful results by relying on its own abilities in solving the problems of the present world.

This need not have led men away from God; for it is God, in his almighty power and wisdom, who created the natural order and laws man has made subservient to his needs. God himself had inserted his plan and ordinances into creation in the form of natural laws; and he continuously sustains this order. Man does not make the natural order, but only discovers it so as to use it for his purposes. All he can ever do is to follow gropingly the steps of divine wisdom and assent to God's pre-ordained laws. Only in the service of the Creator can he fulfil the biblical injunction to rule the earth. Our own scientific and technological age could, on these lines, have led to a natural knowledge of God of increasing range and depth.[38]

Instead of this, the wealth of discoveries, such as atomic power, and scientific achievements like the orbiting of satellites, have served to intoxicate men and induce a kind of blindness to God. In discovering God's laws of nature and applying them, they act as if they themselves had made these laws and had no

---

[38] Cf. F. Dessauer, *Prometheus und die Weltübel*, Frankfurt, 1959.

use for God; they are misled about their own nature, the meaning of life, and lose all certainty. The power they have won has become a menace to all life on earth.

The renewal of faith has to take account of this problem of modern man and the scientific age. It will be the triumph of faith to show man the meaning of his life. A strongly rooted faith is needed to teach modern man to come to terms with himself and his neighbour, to make the forces of nature serve, and not overwhelm, mankind.

2. Reform of morals

Pope John XXIII designated one of the main objects of the Council as "the salutary moral renewal of the Christian people". Men today are no worse than those of previous generations, but they are exposed to greater dangers. No doubt, in earlier times—the Renaissance, for example—there was a decline in Christian moral conduct and gross corruption in public life; but this was confined to a small circle and did not affect the people at large. Today, however, immoral principles and practices are brought to the attention of all through radio, cinema, television, newspapers, and no one is immune. These media of mass influence raise new pastoral problems, for they can be put to good use, and, in fact, often are. There is a picture of Dürer's, "Knight, Death and Devil", which shows a man passing triumphantly through all the dangers of this world. But today the destructive powers of darkness have so many features and shapes, they lurk in so many points of vantage, that it has become inordinately difficult for anyone, however prepared, to avoid contamination and defilement.

The sense of purity and uprightness in both private and public life needs to be stirred up anew. Once the rising generation acknowledges purity of morals in the spirit of faith as a positive value, the signs of decadence we see around us, the fruit of a philosophy based solely on the passions, will disappear more quickly than we might now imagine. The Council will initiate a new springtime of Christian living with its source in the teachings of faith, and rekindle among men the love of Christ. The Spirit of God is still mighty enough today to renew the face of the earth.

Those who speak about the reform of morals must never forget that it can only come from the spirit of the Gospel, from faith in the Redeemer crucified and risen. In taking account of the changes around us, we must never assimilate ourselves to the world in its estrangement from God. Living in the world, we work for the coming of the kingdom of God, who came to us as a child in the crib at Bethlehem. The Council will prepare the way for the kingly rule of Christ, so splendidly portrayed in the Christmas liturgy. All who believe in the Incarnate Son of God, born on that holy night, can and should work, from now on, in preparing for the Council. As Pope John XXIII said, in his encyclical *Ad Petri Cathedram:* "The success of the coming Ecumenical Council will depend more on the great ardour of your concerted prayers, vying, as it were, with each other in holy rivalry, than on any human efforts, care and industry. And we extend also a warm invitation to those who are not of this fold, yet who reverence and worship God and strive in all sincerity to obey his commandments, may they too join in this prayerful appeal to God."

VII

The Unity of the Church and the Question of Reunion

One factor in the new world-situation is the pre-emptory call for the unity of all Christians. The Holy Father always speaks of the Church's catholicity as bound up with her unity, and emphasizes, in the same connection, that unity by no means implies uniformity. Unity of worship admits all the riches of the western and eastern liturgies; unity of doctrine is consistent with the different approaches of the western and eastern schools of theology, and unity of government respects the special characteristics of individual regions with their time-honoured traditions. This variety in unity was well brought out by the present Pope in his encyclical *Ad Petri Cathedram,* and he intends the Council to demonstrate convincingly this same truly comprehensive unity. Addressing the diocesan presidents of Italian Catholic Action, he said: "The Ecumenical Council is itself a testimony to world-wide catholicity of unusual and far-reaching significance. The course of events shows clearly that this project to further the salvation of man was due to God's grace. For the idea of the Council was not the fruit of long premeditation, but the sudden flowering of an unexpected spring ... With God's grace, then, we will hold this Council; we desire to prepare for it by considering carefully what, in the life of Catholics, stands in greatest need of being restored and strengthened, according to what we have learnt of our Lord. When we have carried out this arduous work and eliminated all that, in the human sphere, might prevent rapid progress, we will present the Church in all her splendour, *sine macula et ruga* (without mark or stain) and say to all who are separated from us, Orthodox and Protestants: 'Look, brethren, this is the Church of Christ. We have striven hard to remain true to her, to beseech the Lord for grace that she may always remain as he willed her to be. Come, then; this is the way opening for your return home. Come and take your place or, rather, retake it, for, for many of you, it was your fathers' place.' What joy, what fruit even in the civil and social spheres may the whole world expect from religious peace, from the restoration of the Christian family!"[39]

[39] *Herder-Korrespondenz* 14, (1959-60), col. 7-8.

1. The question of reunion

This makes us realize the Pope's constant loving attitude to the separated Christians, inviting them to see the Church as their home, where they will repossess themselves of all true Christian values. In returning to their home, they will not have to forego any of the Gospel teaching or of the devotion they already possess, God's gift to them, but whose source and native land is the Catholic Church. Cardinal Newman, looking back on his life, wrote in a letter : "What else can I say but that the great luminous truths I received as a child from evangelical teaching, have been imprinted on my heart more and more strongly by the holy Roman Church! The Church has added to the simple evangelistic instructions of my first teachers, but has in no wise diminished, weakened or diluted them".[40] This is what the Pope means when he repeatedly assures those outside the Church that she is no alien thing, but their true home. He says in his encyclical of 29th June, 1959 : "The coming Council will surely be a sublime manifestation of truth, unity and love. May those who are separated from this Apostolic See, beholding this manifestation of unity, derive from it the inspiration to seek out that unity which Jesus Christ prayed for so ardently from his heavenly Father."

The Pope personally addresses all separated Christians in words of love and solicitude. "May this wonderful manifestation of unity by which the Catholic Church stands out unique and resplendent, may the desires and prayers by which she implores from God the same unity for all mankind, exert a saving influence upon your minds and hearts—yes, *your* minds, for we are speaking now to those of you who are separated from this apostolic see. Indulge this love we bear you, and let us call you sons and brothers. Permit that in our fatherly and loving heart we cherish the hope for your return . . . observe, we beg of you, that when we lovingly invite you to the unity

[40]John Henry Newman: Letter of 24 Feb., 1887.

of the Church, we are inviting you not to the home of a stranger, but to your own, your Father's, house. It belongs to you all. We long for you 'in the bowels of Jesus Christ'; permit, then, that we appeal to you to remember your fathers 'who have spoken the word of God to you; whose faith follow, considering the end of their conversation' (Heb.13 : 7). We seem to see the illustrious company of the saints in heaven inviting you by the example of their lives to this same unity. Your own nations sent them on before you into heaven. Many of them bequeathed to you in their writings an authentic and lucid explanation of the teachings of Jesus Christ. They invite you once more to union with this Apostolic See, with which for many centuries your Christian communities were once happily united." (*Ad Petri Cathedram*).

2. *The present urgency of reunion*

The Pope lays stress on the fact that many of those outside the Church have a sincere love of truth, which has already overcome many prejudices against the Church, and praises them for it. In the ecumenical movement he sees a longing on the part of non-Roman Chritianity for "at least some form of unity".

Dr. Visser't Hooft, the general secretary of the World Council of Churches, asks "what is the unity we ought to consider as corresponding to the common vocation of the Churches. Now it is clear that, on account of our separation, we cannot at present agree on what faith and Church order require for full union. Certainly it is not the case that we hold nothing in common as to the essence of Christian unity. In the short history of the ecumenical movement we have already been able to give common assent to a number of important factors of this matter. It seems as if, through our common striving to understand what the New Testament says on the essence of unity in Christ, we will be led on to further common convictions ... First of all, we turn to our Lord's sacerdotal prayer in the seventeenth chapter of St John. We have so often heard the words, 'that they all may be one', that we hold their meaning to be self-evident, whereas we ought to ask what they mean in the context of the whole prayer ... Next we find that the most detailed teaching on unity is given in the form of a prayer. That means that the unity to which we are called is one that we receive and do not make ourselves ... Our prayer is for the renewal of unity where it exists, and its restoration where it has been lost. Here we have to bear in mind that the unity described has three different aspects or dimensions. There is that of height—the vertical dimension, which applies to the unity of the Son and his flock with the Father; that of length —the horizontal dimension of time, which applies to the unity of the apostles with those who, afterwards, come to believe in Jesus; that of breadth, the horizontal dimension of space, which applies to the unity of those who, in all countries, follow the one Lord ... Unity encompasses the world and aims at including the dispersed children of God everywhere. The prologue of St John's Gospel already strikes this note of universality: 'But as many as received him, he gave them power to be made the sons of God, to them that believe in his name'. This theme is pursued in the parable of the Good Shepherd : Other sheep there are, who are to be brought into one fold under one shepherd ... The words 'that the world may believe that thou hast sent me' can only mean that there is here something visible, and that this unity will be manifested in a way which is sufficiently unusual to the world's sight and hearing as to make men see and hear. If it is to convince them, this unity must clearly contrast with the many familiar kinds of unity, social, political, national, cultural, ideological. It must be one inexplicable by the usual motives impelling men to unity. It must transcend obstacles that are apparently insurmountable. It must make men ask what is the unknown power that brings men together in spite of their separateness. It must point to the One who gathers his people from all races and nations. Consequently, it is entirely wrong to consider the spiritual unity of John, Chapter 17, as invisible, as a Platonic ideal or a noble feeling in the depths of the believer's soul, without concrete expression in a common life and witness. The world must be brought to believe on the ground of this unity of the Church, and through it acknowledge what God has done in Christ. But this becomes impossible if unity remains either an abstract idea or a secret conviction in men's hearts. The unity that reflects the communion of the Father and the Son must be manifested on earth in the actual life of the Church, her message and external ordering, in the mutual relations of her members, and in her collective action in the world ... Unity in Christ demands visible expression. To say that disunity can be conquered through invisible unity, while we continue living in actual disunity, is as unreasonable as to say we can conquer our sins invisibly, while continuing to commit them. The error consists in denying that the Church must show forth her unity concretely in perceptible forms. We have seen too that the same holds good of the Church's witness in the mission fields; her unity is bound up with her witness to her Lord's power and love. Church unity means unity in whatever is essential to her life : a common faith, common sacraments, common worship, common life in every place where the Church is set up."[41]

The Holy Father is conscious how urgently the present time calls for unity among Christians. The rapid growth of the populations of Asia and Africa means that ever greater numbers are alien to the Church and do not believe in Christ. Yet Christ himself commanded us to gain all peoples for him. The greatest obstacle to this end is the division among

[41]W. A. Visser't Hooft, *Unter dem einen Ruf, Eine Theologie der ökemenischen Bewegung*,Stuttgart, 1940, pp. 80-92.

Christians. Their division into numerous confessions is a scandal, not only to the Asians and Africans, but to the de-christianized masses of Europe with their avowed hostility to Christianity. Successful evangelization and vigorous missionary work demands, as a necessary condition, the concentration of all Christian forces in a single community bearing one and the same witness to Christ.

3. The necessity of visible unity

It is not enough for separated Christians to respect each other and meet in a spirit of charity. This very charity of theirs should make them seek visible unity in the one Church of Christ. The Roman Catholic Church has preserved such a unity in spite of all the divisions that have occurred. No doubt the splendour and force of this unity were lessened in the eyes of the world by the breakaway of the Eastern Church and by the Reformation, but unity still remains in the *Una Sancta Catholica et Apostolica Ecclesia.*

Nor is it enough to postpone the achievement of unity of all Christians to the end of the world, and to say that the unity of the Church is an eschatological gift, or to put forward the "branch theory" that the different Christian confessions are branches of the tree which is the one Church. Finally, it is not enough to claim a hidden unity and to say that all who believe in Christ as God and Redeemer are already invisibly one, and we must be satisfied with that.

Christ undoubtedly willed a visible unity. Christianity in its origin, the Church of the first age, formed a visible unity in the doctrines of faith, in worship, in government. Ignatius of Antioch, Irenaeus of Lyons, Cyprian of Carthage, Augustine and the great doctors of the east gave this visible unity theological formulation, and the ecumenical Councils aimed at protecting or restoring it. The scandal of visible separateness and division cannot be conjured away by appealing to an invisible unity. What sort of impression could it possibly make on the non-Christian world? The world sets store on what it sees, and what it sees at present is a Christendom split up into many separate bodies. Nothing short of the visible unity willed by Christ can prove to the world that we are all children of the one heavenly Father, brothers and sisters of Jesus Christ. All have the duty of seeking this unity, in obedience to the Lord of the Church. In his sacerdotal prayer Christ besought the Father "that they may be one in us, that the world may believe that thou hast sent me" (John 17 : 21). Only in this spirit can we work fruitfully for reunion according to the will of Christ and by the means he desires.

4. *The ecumenical Council and the unity of Christendom*

One of the main objects of the Council is to prepare the way for this unity. Our own Church has, indeed, kept unity, but it has to bring into it those outside. The *catholicity* of the Church means its ability to take in and validate all that is true and good according to the will of Christ.

What may we expect from the Council as regards this search for ways to reunion? Our answer is simple. At this turning-point in her history, the Church will bring out her intrinsic catholicity in a more striking and convincing way. This catholicity is unity in essentials, liberty in the approved variations in liturgy, theology and canon law, the whole being subject in charity to the Lord and Head of the Church, Jesus Christ, and his visible representative, the pope. It is the work of the Council to make known this catholicity in all its breadth and to express the many aspects of the mystery of our redemption in the Church's teaching and life.

The way to reunion is long and hard. We must not underestimate the doctrinal differences that keep Protestants and Catholics apart. Obedience to God's word and loyalty to the truth prevent mutual respect and charity from making us bypass the question of what is true or false. Naïve optimism is as much to be avoided as hopeless pessimism. The right attitude is one of Christian hope, which trusts to the working of the Holy Spirit and, at the same time, does not lose sight of the fact of separation so rooted in history. This is what the Pope means when he says: "The greatest hopes have been stirred up by the simple yet highly significant fact of the proclamation of a Council. No doubt this important event will not remove at a single stroke all the factors which make for the existing separation of Christians from one another. Our hope must be centred in God and the abundance of his grace, which will surely be given us."

CHAPTER SIX

The Pope's Pentecost Message and the Preparations for the Second Vatican Council

In the Encyclical Letter *Ubi arcano* of 23rd December, 1922, Pius XI expressed his wish and intention "to continue the ecumenical Council for which Pius IX, the Pope of our youth, had prepared a wide field of work, but had only been able to achieve a part, albeit one of importance". Pius XI besought God for some "manifest sign" when it should be summoned, and, both in this and various subsequent encyclicals, laid out a kind of programme for the future Council, which he himself was not able to bring about.[1]

We may note certain important points of agreement between Pius XI's plan and that of the present Pope.

1. Pius XI had prepared and hoped for an ecumenical Council from the beginning of his pontificate. But he waited for a "manifest sign" from the Lord of the Church; he waited for the time, hidden from him, that God had decided and appointed.[2] The sign Pius XI longed for was given to John XXIII, who spoke in these terms: "We have proclaimed the ecumenical Council in obedience to an inspiration which we

---

[1] Ermenegildo Lio O.F.M., "Pio XI ed il Concilio Ecumenico" in: *Osservatore Romano*, 22nd April, 1960, p. 4.

[2] Cf. the Bull summoning the Council of Trent, 22nd May, 1542 . . . *Quam voluntatem dum exspectamus, dum observamus tempus absconditam, tempus beneplaci tui, o Deus* (Psalm 68: 14).

felt directly given in the humility of our heart as a sudden, un-expected motion". "The idea of the Council did not come to maturity as the fruit of long consideration, but was rather the spontaneous flowering of an unexpected spring."[3]

2. Pius XI expressly stated that the Council he planned should be a continuation of the Vatican Council. Both in the encyclical *Ubi arcano* and in subsequent encyclicals he put forward certain subjects which suggested a programme for the intended Council, and recalled the proposals, plans and *schemata* of the Vatican Council.[4] All that he said in this connection was dominated by two main considerations—the unity of the Church and her catholicity. Pius XI laid particular emphasis on the participation of the laity, in unity with their bishops and obedience to their instructions, in the hierarchical apostolate of the Church. In addition, he required unity of action by bishops, priests and laity in the defence of Christian truth against present-day errors, both speculative and practical; their refutation had already been taken in hand by the Vatican Council. He intended that the Council he was anxious to promote should pursue further the theological matters projected in the programme of the Vatican Council. Catholic doctrine should be expounded, and errors refuted.[5] Pius XI worked out a whole doctrinal programme, "which, in its teaching on the Church, the pope and the episcopate, continues that of the Vatican Council, and, in the Church's moral and social teaching, the subsequent papal pronouncements".[6] He expounded the catholicity of the Church especially in his missionary encyclical *Rerum Ecclesiae* (1926) and many discourses.[7]

It is the wish of John XXIII that the coming Council should

---

[3] *Herder-Korrespondenz* 1958-59, p. 413. *Osservatore Romano*, 11th August, 1959, p. 1.
[4] E. Lio, *loc. cit.* p. 4; Th. Granderath, *loc. cit.*, Vol. I, pp. 13-19; 27-45; 6-56; 434-453; Vol. II, pp. 79-108; 249-253.
[5] E. Lio, *loc. cit.*, p. 4, col. 1.
[6] *Ibid.*
[7] Encyclical *Rerum Ecclesiae*, AAS, XVIII (1926), 65ff.

be called the Second Vatican Council. He has not said any
thing about it being a formal continuation of the first. Thirty
eight years have passed since the encyclical *Ubi arcano,* and
ninety since the Vatican Council. It is true that the Council
of Trent was interrupted by intervals of three and even of more
than ten years, but the continuation of a Council after ninety
years would be unprecedented in history. Calling the future
Council the Second Vatican does not simply mean that its dis
cussions on doctrinal matters are to be taken up again at the
point where they were left by the first. Cardinal Tardini has
pointed out that the discussions of the coming Council will not
be "predominantly dogmatic".[8] Nonetheless, since the Council
has to refute errors, and the warped ideologies of the present
day are but the development of the errors prevailing at the
time of the Vatican Council, in practice the new Council would
be a continuation of the earlier, as we see to have been tradition
ally the case with all the Councils. The present Pope's encycli
cals *Ad Petri Cathedram* and *Princeps pastorum* develop the
main themes of his pontificate up to now, the unity and the

---

[8]Cf. Yves Congar, "Konzil und Ökumene", in: *Trierer Theol. Zeitschrift*
Vol. 69 (1960), p. 139: "Everything indicates that the coming Council will
have a strong pastoral orientation. We are thinking of the orientation of
John XXIII's pontificate, of the urgent problems arising everywhere, and of
the circumstance that the Council has been preceded by a Roman diocesan
synod. This synod impressed all the members of the Roman Congregation
and of the Curia, who will of course play an essential role in the preparation
for the Council, with its wholesome atmosphere of purely pastoral concern
I personally incline to the view that this Council, dominated by the question
of unity and by the problems of pastoral and missionary work, will only
consider those doctrinal subjects which are closely bound up with ecumenical
pastoral and missionary problems. The Vatican Council approached the
question of the relations between faith and science—the nineteenth century
problem—from a very intellectual or, if you like, doctrinal, standpoint. I
saw itself faced with the early formulations of modern rationalism, then a far
reaching social, or we might say mass, reality. The Council considered, on the
whole, only its philosophical causes, that is, a particular use of the intellect
These causes are real enough; but to-day we are far more conscious of the
decisive importance of its social causes. There can, therefore, be no doubt
the Council will consider these questions, and confront the present generation
with all that faith demands in a very positive, evangelical and apostolic
fashion."

catholicity of the Church. That gives us an indication of the programme of the coming Council.

3. In the encyclical *Ubi arcano* in which he announced the continuation of the Vatican Council, Pius XI also treated of the reuniting of the separated Christian bodies. John XXIII, on his first announcement of the Council, described as one of its functions the invitation to the separated brethren to seek that unity of the Church Christ willed.[9]

When John XXIII, on the 25th January, 1959, announced a forthcoming ecumenical Council, he aroused both a world-wide interest and immense hopefulness. The President of the General Assembly of the United Nations, Dr. Malik, himself a Lebanese and a member of the Greek Orthodox Church, said that the Council could "with its limitless possibilities" be the most important event of the twentieth century, the most important, even, for many centuries.

I

The Conclusion of the First Stage of Preparation

There are two things which have caused astonishment far beyond ecclesiastical circles :

1. The profound interest and welcome of the public throughout the world at this announcement. This was hardly to be expected at a time which abounds in sensational events. It is an expression of the longing of separated Christians for unity so powerful that no one can ignore it. Quite understandably, the word "ecumenical" gave rise at first to many mis-

---

[9]Cf. E. Lio, *loc. cit.*, col. 2-5.

understandings; but it was soon clear to all that it was a question of an assembly of Catholic bishops from all parts to treat of matters of faith and morals, in union with the Pope and under his direction.

2. The second is the speed of preparations for the Council, the results of which could be seen only a few months later. By the end of October, 1959, eighty per cent of all the bishops had already sent their proposals for the subjects to be discussed to the Commission charged with the first preparation.

At Whitsun 1960, Pope John XXIII, in his *Motu Proprio, Superno Dei nutu,* brought to an end the work of the *Commissio antepreparatoria* of the Council, which he had set up a year before. It had been presided over by Cardinal Tardini, and sent out more than three thousand documents to ecclesiastical superiors, to universities and faculties, and to Roman authorities so as to gain information from the widest possible sources for the preparation of the Council. They went unimpeded to all parts of the world. More than two thousand answers from the Church's hierarchy were received and placed before Roman Congregations of Cardinals, who forwarded to the Pope their own comments and suggestions. In addition, there came some sixty detailed opinions from Catholic universities and faculties.

All these suggestions, opinions and proposals, numerous and detailed though they were, were classified, evaluated and synthesized in only nine months, thanks to the Roman genius for lucidity and comprehension. First, they were all registered and copied, then carefully studied and assessed, and finally classified according to their contents. Their world-wide provenance made it clear what were the most important problems of the individual provinces, countries and missions, and these were brought to the fore in a summary of the collated material. So came into being an extremely useful monograph of about twenty pages which gives a succinct yet comprehensive account of the proposals of bishops from all over the world. In the same way, those of the Roman Congregations were drawn up and evaluated; and, finally, in April those of the various universities.

All this work was done mainly by four priests under the direction of Monsignor Felici, and completed by the beginning of May, 1960. They worked intensively, unaided by electronic computers. Monsignor Felici informed Cardinal Tardini practically every day on the state of the work, and received precise instructions how to proceed.

The Holy Father himself took part personally even in this first stage of the preparations for the Council. Monsignor Felici laid before him the most important proposals of the bishops, the Roman authorities and the universities; and the Pope wrote in the *motu proprio* of 5th June, 1960: "We ourselves followed this work and research, which was carried through with the utmost care. We considered it our duty to read with particular attention the proposals and wishes of the bishops, the suggestions and recommendations of the authorities of the Roman Curia, and the opinions submitted by the universities". The marginal notes in his own hand, giving opinions, references, statistics and general views, will be a standing witness for the future to his close personal direction of the preparatory work.

In all the history of the Church no Council has been prepared with such a comprehensive survey of the views of the episcopate and the authorities concerned. The Holy Father acknowledges, in the *motu proprio* alluded to, his gratitude for the cordial co-operation of his spiritual brothers and sons in the first stages of the preparation. He has ordered that the results of this work and its underlying principles should be published as the first part of the *Acta praeconciliaria*. The Commissions now set up for the immediate preparation can make use of

them in working out the subjects decided on by the Pope for
the Council to deal with.[10]

II

The Setting up of the Preparatory Commissions and the Beginning of Direct Preparation

In the *motu proprio* of 5th June, 1960, the Pope repeats: "We
regard as an inspiration from on high the idea of a Council,
which, from the very beginning of our pontificate, appeared
as the flowering of an unexpected spring. Indeed, the Church,
the beloved bride of Christ, can win new and brighter splendour from such a solemn assemblage of bishops round the
Roman Pontiff in these agitated times. For those who bear the
name of Christians but are separated from this apostolic see, a
new hope shines forth that they will hear the voice of the divine
Shepherd and return to the one Church of Christ". After a
brief survey of the course and conclusion of the first stage of
preparation, the Pope continues: "Now it has become clear,
from the vast quantity of material collected, what are the subjects that the Council has to deal with for the good of the
Church and the salvation of souls. The time has come to start,
with God's help, on the formation of the Commissions for the
study of the subjects to be treated by the Council. They will
consist of Cardinals, bishops and priests eminent in virtue and
learning, from both secular and regular clergy, chosen from
different localities, so that the catholicity of the Church may be
manifested.

---

[10]Cf. "Il primo passo verso il Concilio Ecumenico", in: *Osservatore Romano*,
5th June, 1960.

"In this *motu proprio* we ordain therefore :

1. In order to prepare the second ecumenical Council of the Vatican, there are to be set up "preparatory Commissions" with the duty of studying the subjects chosen by us, so taking account of the wishes of the bishops and the proposals of the authorities of the Roman Curia.

2. The Commissions may each be divided, if need arises, into sections or subcommissions.

3. Each Commission will have a president and a definite number of members. The president will be a cardinal. The members will be chosen from among bishops and distinguished priests.

4. To each of the Commissions will be added consultors chosen from experts in particular fields.

5. Each Commission will have a secretary.

6. The presidents and members of the Commissions, and also the consultors and secretaries, will be chosen by us.

7. Ten preparatory Commissions are appointed. If necessary, more can be set up, as we judge fit. They are as follows :

(a) The theological Commission, with the function of surveying questions concerning scripture, tradition, faith and morals.

(b) The Commissions for bishops and the government of dioceses.

(c) The Commission on discipline of clergy and laity.

(d) The Commission for religious orders.

(e) The Commission for sacramental discipline.

(f) The Commission for the sacred liturgy.

(g) The Commission for studies and seminaries.

(h) The Commission for the eastern Churches.

(i) The Commission for the missions.

(j) The Commission for the lay apostolate, that is, for all questions concerning Catholic Action, religious and social action.

8. In addition, there is appointed a secretariat for dealing with questions about modern means of publicity (press, broadcasting, television, films, etc.). It will be presided over by a prelate named by us, and its members and consultors will also be chosen by us.

9. To show our love and benevolence towards those who have the name of Christians, but are separated from this Apostolic See, and to enable them to follow the work of the Council and to find more easily the way to that unity "for which Christ so ardently besought the heavenly Father", we appoint a special "council" or secretariat to be presided over and organized by a cardinal chosen by us, in the same way as the Commissions.

10. Finally a Central Commission will be formed, over which we will ourselves preside, either personally or through a cardinal designated by us. Its members will be the presidents of the individual commissions, a few other cardinals, and some bishops from different parts of the world.

11. There will be a certain number of advisers added to the Central Commission, chosen from bishops and eminent priests.

12. The Central Commission will have a secretary, who will be at the same time general secretary.

13. The members of the Central Commission, and also the advisers and general secretary will be chosen under our authority.

14. The Central Commission has the function of following the work done by the individual Commissions, and, if necessary, bringing them into accord. It will communicate the results to us, so as to enable us to determine the subjects to be dealt with in the ecumenical Council. The Central Commission will also propose rules for the procedure of the forthcoming Council.

15. Finally, secretariats will be established to see to the technical matters connected with holding the Council."[11]

---

[11] Motu proprio *Superno Dei Nutu.*

III

A Comparison with the Preparatory Commissions of the First Vatican Council

These preparatory commissions now set up are modelled, as a comparison will show, on those of the first Vatican Council. There too was a directive central commission, to which were joined the following commissions for particular matters : one for doctrine, one for religious orders, one for Church discipline, one for the eastern Churches and the missions, and one for questions relating to the Church and politics. Their constitution originated from a proposal submitted by Cardinal Bizarri to the preparatory commission for advising on the business of the Council on 10th May, 1865. The Cardinal took the view that, in the preparation of the Council, men were needed who were not only learned and prudent, but also familiar with the principles laid down by the Holy See. These qualities were not likely to be found conjoined in a single person, and so a number of specialists would have to be employed. The Cardinal pointed out that the Roman Congregations had many members who, besides being familiar with their special field, were also steeped in the Roman tradition and had the necessary competence in administration. They ought, therefore, to form the basic membership of the preparatory commissions. To them should be added eminent theologians and canonists from various countries and nations, whose theoretical knowledge would be valuable in the discussions.

The commissions were, in fact, formed on these principles. Pope Pius IX invited both the nuncios and the bishops everywhere to make suggestions for the summoning of foreign consultors. When these were first chosen, some dissatisfaction was expressed that they came from too small a circle, and so additional ones well-known for their learning were summoned; their acumen and their familiarity with the theological tendencies and religious situation of their respective countries would be of great value. "Thus we see, for example, on the directing commission the learned canonist of Louvain, Faye, and the celebrated historian, Hefele. The latter especially, as the historian of the Councils, was able to use his expert knowledge of the Councils of many centuries in a Congregation that had to make all the dispositions for the holding of the Council." So wrote Granderath,[12] who went on to enumerate other foreign theologians, historians and canonists, such as Alzog, Hettinger, Hergenröther, whose intimate knowledge of their countries and of Protestant theology proved of great service.

The commissions set up by the Pope at Whitsun 1960 should correspond, more or less, in their structure to those which prepared the first Vatican Council. In both cases there is a like relationship to the Roman Congregations, whose prefects are also presidents of most of the present commissions. Cardinal Ottaviani is president of the theological commission, Cardinal Mimmi that of the commission for bishops and diocesan administration. Cardinal Ciriaci will preside over the commission for ecclesiastical discipline, Cardinal Valeri over that for the regular clergy, Cardinal Aloisi Masella over that for the sacraments, Cardinal Pizzardo over that for studies and seminaries. Cardinal Cicognani will have the presidency of the commission for the eastern Churches, and Cardinal Cento that of the commission for the lay apostolate.

A closer comparison between the preparatory commissions of the two Councils reveals certain differences due to altered circumstances and new problems. Instead of five commissions,

---

[12]Th. Granderath, *loc. cit.*, Vol. I, pp. 81-2.

there are now ten, with the addition of two secretariats. The field of each commission is more specialized, and some subjects are new, such as the lay apostolate, whose formation was due to the urgent needs of the present day. We must note too the setting up of a special commission for seminaries and their studies, which will doubtless carry further the directives of the Bull *Deus scientiarum* of May 1931. In the former Council a single commission dealt with questions both of the eastern Churches and the missions. There is now a commission for each, with a wide range of fresh problems to consider.

In the former Council, the doctrinal commission held the first place, as does now the commission for theological questions under Cardinal Ottaviani. It has always been recognized that all reform measures in the Church are closely dependent on doctrinal teaching, This is clearly exemplified in the Council of Trent. The emperor Charles V desired a purely reforming Council and the postponement of all doctrinal questions. But Pope Paul III and his advisers realized that the differences with the Protestants were not confined to purifying the Church and renewing Christian life, but that the Catholic faith must be clearly defined and safeguarded before real measures of reform could be adopted. It was therefore determined that each session should treat concurrently questions of faith and reform, with priority for the former. It is highly probable that the present commission for theological questions will continue the work of the two preceding Councils on scripture and tradition, the relation of the sacraments to the Church, and the formation of the theology of the Church.

IV

The Secretariats and the Concerns of Christianity

The two secretariats represent something new in conciliar history. Constantly the wish has been expressed that reliable information should be forthcoming from press, radio and television about the preparations for the Council. The Church is well aware of the importance of these media of publicity; they are much more powerful in forming opinion than anything was ninety years ago. The establishment of a special secretariat for the purpose is a decision made all the more readily in that the press and wireless of nearly all countries have taken a friendly interest in the prospect of a Council. This is in striking contrast with the press at the time of the first Vatican Council, when it was mainly antagonistic. We may therefore hope that the new secretariat will work to keep alive interest in the Council and to ensure that its discussions and decisions are properly understood.

Still more important is the establishment of a secretariat for furthering the unity of all Christians (*Secretariatus ad unitatem christianorum fovendam*). The Holy Father has entrusted the direction of this work to Cardinal Bea, whose experience in biblical research and teaching and profound knowledge of the theologies of the separated communities qualify him pre-eminently for its many duties and has appointed Dr. J. G. M. Willebrands, formerly Professor of Philosophy at Warmond Holland, as Secretarial Director of the Bureau. Cardinal Bea has been called a conservative reformer, which indicates both his profound attachment to tradition and his awareness of the needs of the present. The formation of the secretariat entrusted to him will be in line with that of the various commissions already enumerated, a fact which serves to emphasize the importance of the new institution. The function of the secretariat is to keep the separated Christians informed about the work of the Council, to study their efforts towards union, and to facilitate their understanding of what the Catholic Church means by unity. The expression *qui christiano nomine decorantur* is something positive, and refers equally to Orthodox, Anglicans and Protestants. It has no pejorative significance which might cause umbrage to Protestants.[13] Any misunderstanding of the sort is ruled out by the Pope's statement that the establishment of the secretariat is a sign of his love and benevolence to the separated brethren.

Interdenominational discussions have been held for decades, and have long been permitted by the well known decree of the Holy Office *De motione oecumenica*. But the desire has often been expressed by both Catholics and Protestants that Rome should have an official body which could give decisive information, receive communications, answer inquiries, and judge the value of efforts made for interconfessional relations. It would also determine the relation of the Catholic Church to the World Council of Churches and the possibility of joint action in, for example, the field of social ethics.[14]

The Holy Father hopes that the new secretariat may help the separated Christians to find the unity for which Christ besought his Father. They all of them seek the unity Christ desired, and are ready to use the means and travel the path indicated by his will. But the effect of different ideas on the Church's nature is that the Orthodox, the Anglicans,

---

[13]Cf. *Materialdienst des Bensheimer Konfessionskundlichen Institutes*, 1959, p. 71.
[14]Cf. the frequent mention in Herder-Korrespondenz. In speaking of "interdenominational discussion", we do not mean to imply that the Catholic Church is a denomination in the sixteenth century meaning of the term.

143

Lutherans and other Protestants also differ on the nature of the unity willed by God and the means to achieve it. The Orthodox view is nearest to the Roman Catholic. That of most of the Protestants is laid down in the seventh article of the Confession of Augsburg : "It suffices for true unity among the Christian Churches that in them the Gospel be preached according to its pure sense and the sacraments administered according to the word of God. And it is not necessary for true unity of the Christian Church that everywhere should be observed the same ceremonies, appointed by men . . ."[15] If this only means that there may be in the Church different theological schools and tendencies, different liturgies and systems of ecclesiastical law, we could well agree. But in fact the same article ascribes the essential structure of the Church, its hierarchical order and the apostolic succession of bishops, as unnecessary, and based on human law. Quite recently, a Lutheran theologian gave it as his opinion that discussions on reunion should be confined to the two central points of preaching and the sacraments, "for the Church is primarily not an institution but a community in belief".

The article just mentioned opened by saying that the Church is the assembly of all the faithful, in which the Gospel is taught in its purity and the sacraments are rightly administered.[16] Bellarmine has already remarked that the question precisely is where the Gospel is rightly understood and the sacraments administered according to the will of Christ. Ignatius of Antioch, Irenaeus of Lyons and Tertullian answered long ago that the episcopate with its apostolic succession was the

---

[15]*Confessio Augustana, Art. VII*, "Die Bekenntnisschriften der evangelisch-Lutherischen Kirche", 3rd. impr. Gottingen 1956, p. 61. The latin text reads : Et ad veram unitatem satis est consentire de doctrina evangelii et de administratione sacramentorum. Nec necesse est ubique similes esse traditiones humanas seu ritus aut ceremonias ab hominibus institutas, sicut inquit Paulus . . . (Eph. 4: 5-6).
[16]*Ibid.*: Est autem ecclesia congregatio sanctorum, in qua evangelium pure docetur et recte administrantur sacramenta.

guarantee of purity of doctrine and right administration of the sacraments in the Church. It is not possible to exclude the questions of the Church's structure as laid down by Christ and of the Church's government from discussions on reunion. They belong to the essence of Church unity, which today occupies the foreground in theological controversy and interconfessional discussions.

<h1 style="text-align:center">V</h1>

How does a Modern Council Work?

How does a modern Council go about its work? Let us take the Vatican Council as an example: the Pope sought the opinion of twenty-one Cardinals residing in Rome and thirty-six Bishops from various countries. The Committee of Cardinals selected the most important of the proposed items and five preparatory sub-committees prepared the doctrinal and disciplinary decrees. Several experts were drawn into these committees from outside to assist with the working out of the proposals, the *Schemata,* for each matter to be discussed. On 27th November, 1869, the agenda was published. The pope as Head of the Council possessed the right of proposing, but bishops could put forward other suggestions whose inclusion was decided on by a *Deputatio de propositis,* appointed by the pope. During the conferences the *Schemata* worked out by the preparatory committees were distributed to the Fathers of the Council, who examined them with their theologians and made their own comments and suggestions, at first orally in the public sessions and then in writing to gain time. Four permanent deputations chosen by the Council, each with twenty-four members, edited the *Schemata* and reformulated them according to the suggestions of the Fathers; this frequently involved a completely new working out, as, for example, in the Constitution on the Faith. Thus improved, the texts were sent back to the Fathers who could again make further suggestions for alteration. After the final shaping of the text by the deputation the *Schemata* were set before the Fathers for approval, at first in successive extracts and then the whole version.

While the first Vatican Council began with six hundred and forty two participants entitled to vote, three times as many can be reckoned on in the coming Council, for there are almost one thousand seven hundred bishoprics and in addition we must include the Cardinals, their Apostolic Vicars, Auxiliary Bishops and religious superiors. This number certainly presents some difficulties in organizing the conferences, but despite the greater number these will be easier to overcome than at the Vatican Council. Technical progress today has made congresses of over two thousand participants a rarity no longer. Very significant is the regulation sent out by Cardinal Tardini that the official language of the Council will be Latin and that there will be no system of simultaneous translation through headphones. The precision and clarity of Latin are such an advantage that the difficulties of fluent self-expression which may arise in individual cases will assume less importance. That it is quite possible to express even problems of this scientific age in Latin has been sufficiently demonstrated.[17] The necessity of thinking clearly and putting vague, dynamic and emotional thoughts in order before expressing them is a salutary discipline imposed by the Latin language, and may well bring useful results.[18]

---

[17]Cf. A. Bacci, "Lexicon eorum vocabulorum quae difficilius latine redduntur", 3rd. impr., Rome, 1955; C. Egger, *Tirolensia Latina*, Innsbruck, 1960.

[18]Antonio Cardinale Bacci, "In quale lingua si parlerà nel Concilio Ecumenico Vaticano II?" in: *Osservatore Romano*, 3rd July, 1960, p. 3.

CHAPTER SEVEN

The Spiritual Condition of Christendom on the Eve of the Council

I

The Problem of the Separated Christian Bodies

THE medieval Church never resigned itself to the separation of the Eastern Church from the west, but constantly, in all sorts of ways, worked for reunion, until the Council of Florence, at any rate for a short time, brought practically the whole of Christendom back to the unity of the visible Church.

Since the Reformation the religious divisions in the west have gone on increasing. Of the 820 million Christians throughout the world, about 440 million are Catholic, 170 million Orthodox, 160 million Protestant, and 50 million Anglican. Never have these divisions been so keenly felt on all sides as they are today. The longing for unity finds visible expression in the ecumenical movement, and has already brought together, in great part, the various Christian communities, apart from the

Roman Catholic Church, in the World Council of Churches.

Christendom now presents a quite different aspect from the Christendom of the pre-Tridentine Councils. Even in the later Middle Ages Christendom was understood as consisting of the Catholics of the entire universe, and the separation of the Eastern Church was believed to have been permanently overcome in the Councils of Lyons and Florence. If today we understand by Christendom all who confess the divinity of Christ and his redemption, it presents a number of divisions, humanly speaking incurable. Yet there is one point on which all are agreed; all seek after the unity willed by Christ. The importance of this is far from negligible; it is the source of the impulse behind the ecumenical movement. It should lead our separated brethren to an understanding of the Catholic idea of unity, as developed by the present Pope in his first encyclical *Ad Petri Cathedram*. Although the reformed Churches have a different conception of unity, it will be possible for them to admit that, as the Catholic Church is convinced that the primacy of Peter's successor, the apostolic succession, and the hierarchical structure of the Church derive from the will of Christ in founding the Church, her understanding of unity, both visible and invisible, is determined accordingly. They will, likewise, see that the Pope's aim in calling the Council is not to bring about union, for which the time is not yet ripe, but, as he insists, to prepare the way for union in the future by renewing the life of the Church. This is the meaning of the following passage in his first encyclical. "That there may be one fold and one shepherd (John 10 : 16). This irresistible assurance was the compelling motive which led us to announce publicly our resolve to call an Ecumenical Council. Bishops will come together there from every corner of the world to discuss important matters of religion. But the most pressing topics will be those which concern the spread of the Catholic faith, the revival of Christian standards of morality, and the bringing of ecclesiastical discipline into closer accord with the needs and conditions of our times. This in itself will provide an outstanding example of truth, unity and love. May those who are separated from this Apostolic See, beholding this manifestation of unity, derive from it the inspiration to seek out that unity which Jesus Christ prayed for so ardently from his heavenly Father."

It is well known that both Orthodox and Protestants were invited to the first Vatican Council. At the time, many bishops hoped that the Council might possibly bring about a reunion of Christendom, a union of the Orthodox Churches with the Roman Catholic, and even the return of Protestant communities to Catholic unity. In September 1868, Pius IX addressed an Apostolic Brief "to all bishops of the eastern rite who are not in union with the apostolic see", and asked them to end the split between east and west, and to come to the ecumenical Council, as their predecessors did to those of Lyons and Florence. Unfortunately this Brief appeared in the Press before it was delivered to the eastern patriarchs; and when the vicar apostolic handed it to the patriarch of Constantinople, the latter replied that he would certainly have accepted and studied it carefully, had he not already seen its contents in the papers. In fact, he said, it put forth claims the Orthodox Church could not admit, and if the bishops had come to the Council the old theological quarrels would have revived, the old wounds reopened, and the existing differences made more acute; the only possible basis for union consisted of the doctrines and customs prevailing before the schism. The patriarch returned the Brief unopened.

II

Eastern Christians and their Hopes for the Council

The significance of the friendly attitude of the Patriarch of
Constantinople and the Orthodox generally to the proclamation of the Council is seen when we compare it with the sharp
refusal of the Orthodox Patriarchs in the case of its predecessor.[1] Pope John's appeal for unity made the Christmas after
his election, to the eastern Christians especially, and the
announcement soon after of an ecumenical Council, made a
deep impression in the Orthodox Churches; and Athenagoras,
the Patriarch of Constantinople, in his response, expressed
their longing for the unity desired by the Lord of the Church.
The note of joyful accord and personal regard for the Pope
turned men's minds for the moment from all those theological
and extra-theological obstacles that still prevent closer contact
and union with Rome. The difficulties that emerged during the
first Vatican Council remain practically unchanged, and in
addition serious differences, both theological, through the
influence of Protestantism and non-theological, through political developments, have arisen since.[2] A special problem arises

---

[1]Fr. D. Wyels, O.S.B., "Le Concile du Vatican en l'Union" in: *Irenikon*,
1929, pp. 489-499; Mansi, *loc. cit.*, Vol. XL, col. 378-416; Th. Granderath,
loc. cit., Vol. I, pp. 303-327.

[2]Cf. P. Gualbertus Mateucci, O.F.M., "De historico faustoque conventu
occidentis cum oriente christiano", in: *Antonianum*, 1960, pp. 293-322; P.
Bernhard Schultze, "Heilige Schrift und Uberlieferung in Verbindung mit
dem Ökumenischen Konzil in der Lehre der byzantinisch-slawischen Theologie",
in: *Ostkirchliche Studien*, Vol. IX, 1960, pp. 3-25; P. Stephanou, S.J., "Il
Patriarcato di Constantinopoli di fronte al problema dell'unione", in Civiltà
Cattolica, 1960, pp. 46-58; K. Algermissen, *Konfessionskunde*, Paderborn, 1957,
pp. 472-525, 899-903.

from the various conceptions of the separated eastern Churches of the nature of ecumenical Councils and of the precise relation of the bishops assembled in Council to the whole Church.[3] Faced with so many problems, external and internal, the separated eastern Churches are making determined efforts in the first place to overcome their differences. The fact that they almost unanimously recognize the leading position of the Patriarch of Constantinople is an indication of the way to unity which appeals to them. In the spring of 1960, the Patriarch Athenagoras paid an official visit to the three other Patriarchs of the Near East, a thing unprecedented in the Byzantine and Turkish eras. The Patriarch of Constantinople was concerned not only with returning their previous visit to himself, but with strengthening the bonds between the Orthodox Patriarchs and preparing the Orthodox Churches for the Prosynod of Rhodes. This meeting was to lead the way to a General Council of the Orthodox Churches which would further their co-operation with one another and lead to closer relations with the Monophysite and Nestorian communities whose differences over the creed of Chalcedon are now for the most part superficial. Will this Council also deal with the relations of the separated Churches with Rome? At most, only in unofficial discussions.[4] At the same time, the activity of the Orthodox Churches in the World Council of Churches will be reviewed in order to bring about a "symphony" of all Christian communities. The Prosynod will now meet towards the end of

---

[3]Gualbertus Mateucci, *op. cit.*, pp. 306-312: *Orientalium mens de vera oecumenici Concilii natura.* Johannes N. Karmiris, in his outline of the dogmatic teaching of the Orthodox Church, stresses the authority of bishops in the Council, saying that "the Orthodox laity is indeed the preserver and guardian of its orthodoxy and belief, but has no power to formulate it validly and authoritatively. This power belongs exclusively to the ecumenical synod, whose work it is alone, and which is inspired and directed by the Holy Spirit to formulate infallibly and proclaim dogmas". *Die orthodoxe Kirche in griechischer Sicht*, Vol. I, Stuttgart, 1959, p. 93. Cf. Karmiris on the episcopal office and the apostolic succession, *ibid.*, p. 86.
[4]Cf. "Apostolos Andreas", *Vers l'unité chrétienne*, Vol. XIII, 1960, pp. 17-19.

1961, and will be preceded by a conference of Orthodox bishops and theologians at Easter.

What do the Easterns think of Church unity and its mode of achievement? We recall what Archbishop Athenagoras of Thyatira said at the plenary assembly of the World Council of Churches in Lund : "The Orthodox Church confesses it is a matter, not of human learning, but of divine revelation. This is to be found only in the one Catholic and Apostolic Church, to which divided Christianity must find its way, if it really aspires to the unity of the Church."[5]

We share the hope expressed by the Greek Orthodox professor of theology, Vasilios Joannidis, after speaking of the messages of recent Popes to the Easterns and of the fruitful theological discussions held : "All this will surely remove the misunderstandings, the hatred and coldness of the past, and create the necessary climate of love and spiritual closeness, making easier mutual understanding, removal of doctrinal differences and the attainment of unity. First we must love one another purely and simply as individuals and as Churchmen, and surely there will follow agreement on dogmatic questions".

III

The Anglican Church

It would be incorrect to describe the Anglicans simply as Protestants. The Anglican Church is, in fact, along with the Lutheran and Calvinist, a special type of reformed Christianity.

---

[5]For the outstanding differences on the primacy see Fr. Chrysostom, O.S.B., *The Ecumenical Council and the Papacy*, New York, 1960. For the Greek Orthodox attitude to the Council, see "To Vima" by H. Alivisatos in: *Vers l'unité chrétienne*, XII, 1959, pp. 22-24.

Three factors combined to give rise to the reformation in England: Henry VIII's desire to divorce Catherine of Aragon, the opposition on the part of some of the laity to clerical privileges, and the writings of Martin Luther, which circulated in England from 1521 onwards.

Among those who read these was Thomas Cranmer, who, about the year 1530, accepted the Lutheran doctrine of justification by faith alone. In 1535, he was nominated archbishop of Canterbury by the king and consecrated. Henry VIII was a typical renaissance absolute ruler and, in addition, was well instructed in theology. In 1521 he had written the *Assertio septem sacramentorum* against Luther, and received from Pope Leo X the title of *Defensor fidei,* still borne by the English Sovereign. In May 1533, Cranmer declared the king's marriage with Catherine to be null, and his union with Anne Boleyn, contracted in January, valid. Pope Clement VII, in July 1533, pronounced the marriage with Anne invalid, and, in consequence, Henry, on 3rd November, 1534, made himself, by the Act of Supremacy, "Protector and Supreme Head of the English Church and clergy". Apart from that he made no change in doctrine. In 1539, he enacted the Statute of Six Articles against Protestant teachings infiltrating into the country.

It was only in the reign of Edward VI, still in his minority, that Cranmer succeeded in introducing the doctrines and practices of the reformers. In 1549, the Book of Common Prayer, composed by himself, was prescribed for general use as the official liturgical book. Three years later, he drew up a Confession formula in forty-two articles, which, in 1563, were reduced to thirty-nine and added to the official prayer book. They put forward the Bible as the sole rule of faith, and taught justification by faith alone. The only sacraments retained were Baptism and the Lord's Supper. Both transubstantiation and Zwingli's interpretation were rejected. The teaching on the

Eucharist does not seem to exclude an objective, real presence of Christ; its positive content must be drawn from the general tenour of the Anglican liturgy.

The doctrine of the Anglican reformation is nowhere so clearly expressed as in its liturgy, and the Book of Common Prayer is what chiefly holds the Anglican Churches together. The traditional Church year is retained, though the number of saint's days is reduced. A dignified rite for Confirmation, Marriage and Orders is laid down, though these, along with Penance and Extreme Unction are not considered sacraments except by Anglo-catholics. The popularity of the Prayer Book is largely due to its beautiful language and richness of thought.

In the Anglican liturgy almost the whole of the Old and New Testaments is read in the course of the year. Cranmer had a strong conviction of the power of the word of God delivered without commentary, as well as confidence in the insight and zeal of the people.

Queen Elizabeth I of deliberate policy had the Act of Supremacy renewed by Parliament and, at the same time, altered. Instead of "Supreme Head", she was called the "Supreme Authority" of the Church, and it was clearly stated, in the 37th article of the Anglican Confession, that the Sovereign might not "meddle with the ministering of God's word or of the sacraments". The hierarchical constitution and many Catholic forms were retained. The episcopal office, based theologically and canonically on the claim to the apostolic succession, was to remain the foundation of the Elizabethan Church. The Anglican bishop of Salisbury, John Jewel, writing in 1562, made the humanistic principle of Church unity in the first five or six centuries (*Consensus quinquevel sesaecularis*) the basis of his exposition of Anglicanism (*Apologia pro Ecclesia Anglicana*). He attempted to combine the national character of the Anglican Church with the universal validity of the early Church tradition, and in that way indicated the basic theological attitude of the Church of England. Lancelot Andrewes (1555-1626), the official theologian of James I, traced the episcopal office to Christ's assignment of a special dignity to certain of his followers; he was the father of the older Anglo-catholicism. He accepted the sacrificial idea of the Eucharist, and taught that the words of consecration effected a change in the elements of bread and wine. He is still held to-day among Anglicans as an authority of the first rank and as the founder of the *via media* between the Roman Catholic Church and the continental reformation.

Although the Church of England was originally a national Church, it has expanded into the Anglican community of Churches, to which belong all the Anglican bishoprics of the world. This community, embracing some thirty provinces and thirty individual dioceses as well, is held together by the thirty-nine articles of belief, acknowledgment of the Bible and the first four Ecumenical Councils, and respect for the tradition of the Church of the first millennium. The individual Churches all worship in the vernacular, with the result that there are more than two hundred liturgical languages and translations of the Book of Common Prayer. Finally, the different provinces feel a bond of loyalty to the existing archbishop of Canterbury as the chief representative of Anglicanism. His utterances on ecclesiastical questions carry great weight, although his jurisdiction is confined to his own province. He has the right to summon the Lambeth Conference of Anglican bishops; it meets about every ten years, and is the most visible sign of a binding community. It is neither a Council nor a diocesan Synod, but its pronouncements are very influential in the Anglican world.

Doctrinal decisions of the Lambeth Conference can only receive binding force by act of Parliament. The Anglican repugnance to theological dogmatism and confessional obligations opened the way to a multiplicity of opinions, views and tendencies, which, from the time of the Reformation, have brought about increased tensions. There are three principles at work side by side : the Protestant and scriptural (Evangelical or Low Church), the humanistic and rationalistic (Latitudinarian or Broad Church), and the institutional and sacramental (Conservative or High Church). These trends continue today to influence the group of Moderate or Central Churchmen, which has no special theological standpoint, but plays a leading part in Church affairs. This centre-party holds that the unity of the various groups in Anglicanism is preserved through their relation to the one glorified Christ and through the same inner principles of Christian living. The juridical structure and the institution of the "historic episcopate" belong to the *bene esse,* not the *esse,* of the Church. The national Churches, provided they retain communion in faith (*salvo jure communionis in fide*), are free to adopt their own forms of worship, their own constitution and discipline. In this way, there can be one and the same "Catholic Church", not only in the different Anglican groups, but also in the various Christian confessions. It is easy to see what an influence this conception could have in the ecumenical movement.

The evangelical (Low Church) party originated in the eighteenth century, stressing the authority of Scripture against that of the Church, and often against that of reason. The evangelicals emphasize personal experience of salvation, justification by faith, sanctification of the individual and his duty to lead a life of holiness. They tend, in the spirit of the Reformation, to a theocratic idea of the State, and aim at influencing politics and legislation through the "conscience of the Christian nation". In large measure, this is a lay movement, and to it was due the first beginnings of Anglican missionary work.

The Broad Church party adopts, in many respects, a liberal standpoint, one of accommodation to the modern conception of the world. Its roots lie in the latitudinarianism of the seventeenth and eighteenth centuries, which adopted and developed the German theology based on Kant and the positivistic-historical theology of Germany. The modernistic stamp received in the twentieth century was of little importance in itself, but it combined with the basic liberal attitude to promote indifferentism. Broad churchmen achieved considerable results in the domain of social action.

In contrast with the liberal school of Tübingen, the three great New Testament scholars of Cambridge, Lightfoot, Westcott and Hort, defended the New Testament exegesis assailed by Strauss and Renan, giving it fresh support by their own researches. Westcott's critical edition of the New Testament became famous; in 1885 he and Hort collaborated to bring out a second edition.

The Anglo-Catholic section came into prominence through the Oxford Movement of the last century; the "Tracts for the Times" were written to make the clergy realize their apostolic calling and authority. The Movement compelled men to reflect anew on the nature of the Catholic Church, the apostolic succession, and also on the necessity and scriptural basis of the episcopal office. Church, priesthood, sacraments and liturgy all took their place in a coherent theological structure and practice grounded on the Augustinian tradition. The sacrament of penance in the Catholic form was readopted; Mass vestments, incense and candles were used; and new religious communities were founded in accordance with the Roman tradition. Since 1920, the Anglo-Catholics have held annual congresses. Many of them take part in efforts for union with the Roman Catholic Church. Between 1921 and 1925 there were held at Malines, under the leadership of Cardinal Mercier and Lord Halifax, private conversations between prominent Anglicans and Catholics on the possibility of future reunion. They came to an end after discussion on the primacy of jurisdiction and the validity of Anglican orders, on which no agreement could be reached. As is well known, Leo XIII, in 1896, after careful examination, declared invalid the orders given according to the Edward VI Ordinal, on account of defect in form and intention.

Though the Malines conversations failed to achieve the results hoped for, they served to clarify both positions and to promote mutual understanding. Rome cannot consider compromise on her teaching on faith and morals; that would be a betrayal of the witness the Lord of the Church requires from her. But that does not prevent many Anglo-Catholics from viewing the Roman Church with increased sympathy and even reverence. For example, the works of Thornton and of Mascall approximate in an extraordinary degree to Roman Catholic ideas. Mascall's *The Recovery of Unity* (London, 1958) corresponds on many points to the Catholic idea of unity. The Anglican theologian, Oliver Tomkins, who was secretary of "Faith and Order" from 1945 to 1952, and then secretary for the working committee of the World Council for "Faith and Order", expressed himself in these words: "The World Council of Churches has a debt of gratitude to Rome. Rome signifies today a standing commentary on our work which we cannot ignore. For some it is simply a warning of what they should not become, for others it is the persistent temptation to get rid of our intolerable tensions in a unity of some kind at least ... But for us all, despite all the objections we may urge, it is a continual reminder to the Council that, when we speak of unity in Christ, we are not speaking of an abstract ideal, but of something that must find expression in history, in flesh and blood. Whether as warning or encouragement, offence or model (to many of us it is always something of both), Rome stands above all our attempts and strivings as an embodied unity, and is on that account impossible to ignore."

We have to remember, however, that there are still essential differences of doctrine between the Roman Catholic Church and Anglicanism, particularly in regard to the Evangelicals and the Broad Church. Many Anglicans consider the episcopal office as only one of many possible constitutional elements in the Church. For Anglo-Catholics, on the other hand, a Christian community without bishops is no Church in the full sense.

The Anglican reformation retained, more than the Lutheran and Calvinist, positive elements of the tradition of the old Church, and so Anglicanism is closer to the Roman Catholic position. Thus the Anglicans held more firmly than all the other reformed confessions to the Councils of the first millennium and the doctrine of the Fathers. They preserved a pronounced sense of the visible unity of the Church and upheld a structure of the Church based on the episcopate. In general, their theology discountenanced an unrestricted application of the principle of the free interpretation of Scripture, since it paid regard to the tradition of the early Church. In addition, Anglicanism retained more of the liturgical riches of the old Church and many forms of its public worship.

The Anglican Church, through possessing so many and diverse elements, naturally acquired a leading position in the ecumenical movement. Their sense for Church order, tradition and visible unity gave the Anglican leaders a constant stimulus to look for points of contact with other communities. A number of conversations have been held and connections formed between the Anglican and the Orthodox Churches. On 22nd November, 1960, the Archbishop of Canterbury left London for Jerusalem, where he met the Orthodox patriarch and other Church leaders of the Near East, and reaffirmed the close friendship long existing between the Anglican and Orthodox Churches. On the return journey Dr. Fisher visited in Constantinople the Orthodox patriarch, Athenagoras I; and afterwards, on 2nd December, paid a "courtesy visit" in Rome to Pope John XXIII. This was the first time since the Reformation that the chief representative of the Anglican world was able to take the initiative in an act of courtesy and friendly regard to the Pope; and it is significant too that the non-catholic world for the most part welcomed or at least respected the act, and only a small minority gave voice to misgivings.

Before his journey, Dr. Fisher had explained in the Church Assembly that his visit to Rome was a clear proof that the two communities could talk together in love and mutual trust. No one could reasonably see in this courtesy visit more than a "simple expression of the longing of the head of one great Christian community to meet the head of another great Christian community, and to speak with him in cordiality and fraternal love". In a like spirit, Dr. Stockwood, the bishop of Southwark, paid a visit to the Pope at the beginning of his pontificate. In June 1959, Donald Rea, a canon of the Church of England, paid his respects to Pope John, who gave him, at the audience, his own breviary, since he had noticed that the canon's was rather worn. This gesture is typical of the whole attitude of the Pope, who, as Archbishop Heenan has said, has a great predilection for Anglicans, and personally desires extensive collaboration with them, naturally without compromising doctrine.

The Anglican Archbishop's visit recalls Pius XII's reception of the president of the German Evangelical Church, Dr. Dibelius, in January 1956. This visit too, despite its private nature, was of historic importance, for it was the first time since the Reformation that a representative of German Protestantism visited the Pope. Dr. Dibelius spoke of his satisfaction and gratitude for the friendliness of his reception, but no one was deluded about the continuance of the differences that divided them. Still, then as now, such a visit can be said to be a sign of the improved climate of opinion of the two confessions.

Dr. Fisher, when in Rome, pointed out : "For the first time

for four hundred years an archbishop of Canterbury has come officially to Rome not to air his own views or complaints, but solely to show respect to his Holiness, the Pope, in the spirit of courtesy and Christian brotherhood. This visit has become possible because the Pope let it be known that he would receive me in the same spirit of Christian brotherhood".

The reception lasted a good hour, and the Pope showed special interest in Dr. Fisher's visit to the East, recalling Pope Gregory the Great's sending of Christian missionaries to England. He presented the Archbishop with a number of volumes, among them the resolutions of the Roman Synod, his addresses as Patriarch of Venice, and the first volume of preparatory acts for the Ecumenical Council. In addition, he gave him and the accompanying chaplains the medal of his pontificate. Dr. Fisher presented to the Pope a fine picture of the queen's coronation ceremony.

The Archbishop, on the day before his visit to the Vatican, expressly indicated the existing differences, including the non-theological factors making for separation which arise from the nature of the English temperament and are closely bound up with doctrinal differences. He gave as his opinion that "at the root of all separation and division there lies always a question of authority and jurisdiction". There are still obstacles enough on the way to union, but no one who confessed Jesus Christ, the source of authority, teaching and jurisdiction, as his Lord and Master must let these deter him from striving towards union.

The day after his meeting with the Archbishop, the Holy Father addressed a number of cardinals at the conclusion of the retreat given at the Vatican, stressing his "respectful admiration" for the Anglican primate and for his "courageous undertaking". He praised too the "dynamic will" with which the Archbishop strove for the excellent purpose of mutual understanding among Christians. At the same time the Pope indicated that there had been no discussion of dogmatic questions which divided the two Churches and had become more acute with the passage of four centuries. But through personal contacts, exchange of ideas and fraternal discussions the day of full understanding would be brought nearer. For the moment, the Pope concluded, the meeting has shown that, on both sides, there were present courtesy, cordiality and understanding. These are "not unimportant fruits of a frank discussion, and they signify that this is a historic date in the relations between the Catholic and the Anglican Church". Yet we must not draw hasty conclusions or make rash prophecies even though the meeting, just before the Vatican Council, augurs well for the future. The Pope, in fact, described the Archbishop's visit as a "foretaste of the results hoped for from the Council".

Neither Catholics nor Anglicans entertain any illusions about the direct results of a courtesy visit like this. No doubt it means an improvement in the attitude of the confessions to each other and so facilitates theological discussions later on. But it does not herald the beginning of a "summit conference" as some journalists think, nor of conversations on union between the two Churches. A sober appraisal of the facts should keep us from undue optimism.

We owe it to the Anglicans and our other separated brethren as well as to ourselves to be honest in the matter. If false hope were fostered and later found to be deceptive, there would perhaps ensue a severe setback in the creating of a climate of calmness, charity and understanding between the different confessions. But with such a climate it will be easy for the separated bodies to feel that the coming Council is an invitation to them to seek that unity for which Christ prayed to his Father on the eve of his passion.

IV

Protestants and the Unity of the Church

1. The general situation

The attitude of contemporary Protestants to a possible invitation is governed largely by their idea of the nature of the
Church and its unity, and may be expressed in these points :[6]

1. Unity is an essential property of the Church.
2. Therefore reformation theology cannot accept the separation of the Churches as justified.
3. It follows that it is the duty of the separated Churches
to seek unity.
4. The unity of the Churches must be sought for the sake
of the truth, not for any practical reasons.
5. Consequently, any kind of indifferentism in matters of
doctrine must be avoided in seeking unity. This is stressed
especially on the Lutheran side, since the Lutheran communities look on their confessional statements of belief as a *Summa
scripturae,* and, with this prerequisite, accept Scripture as the
norma normans (regulating norm, as opposed to the *norma
normata*) of all doctrinal teaching. From their idea of the
Church as expressed in their confessional statements Protestants dispute the claim of the Catholic Church to be the true
Church of Christ and its demand for the return of the other
Christian communities.
6. From the principles of the Reformation there follows a
theological view of Councils differing in its main lines from the
Catholic. As Altendorf says : "In Protestantism, with its rejection with Luther of the traditional idea of the Church, there

---

[6]Cf. Antoine Wenger, "Le Concile" in: *La Croix,* 31st May, 1960.

was no room for the Roman Catholic idea of Councils, nor indeed for any common understanding of their nature."[7] Luther's views in his "on Councils and Churches" are a denial of the traditional idea of Councils.[8] He reduces the authority of Councils to the principle of *sola scriptura,* interpreting Scripture from the standpoint of his views on justification. Luther recognizes only the four ancient "chief Councils" of Nicea, Constantinople, Ephesus and Chalcedon, on the ground that they rightly express the teaching of Scripture. The early Fathers, however, held that these Councils were true to Scripture because of the assistance of the Holy Spirit preserving the assembly of bishops from error; and it is precisely this basis of the authority of Councils that Luther rejected. This attitude of his corresponds to his idea of the Church; it is not to be attributed to his despair that the Council all desired to see had not yet been summoned. In his view, a Council was a meeting of experts in Scripture, where the sole rule of faith was Scripture as understood by the reformers. As a result, what the Protestants really wanted was not a Council, but a conference on religion.

7. When Pope John XXIII announced the holding of an ecumenical Council, the word "ecumenical" gave rise to a misunderstanding, and it was thought he meant a joint Council. The idea seemed to Protestants strange and repugnant; but they were reassured by Cardinal Tardini's explanation that the Council would deal with internal matters of the Catholic Church. The General Secretary of the World Council of Churches, Dr. Visser't Hooft, said there was no reason to regret that it would be simply an intra-Catholic affair, for it was too early for official discussions on Christian unity. Should an invitation be sent to the World Council of Churches, it would be doubtful about accepting it; but certainly it could take no

---

[7]H. D. Altendorf, "Konzile", in: *RGG* III, col. 1803.
[8]W.A. 50, 509ff.

action officially, since it was not authorized by any of its member-churches to take part in such discussions. Further, it must be remembered that interconfessional discussions were only just beginning, and were restricted to only a few churches in Europe.[9]

Evangelical theologians throughout time regard the question of an invitation to the Council as merely secondary. They are extremely interested in continuing discussions with Catholic theologians, and hope the Council will facilitate contact of the latter with the ecumenical movement and the World Council of Churches so as to find new ways to unity. How to answer any invitation to Protestant leaders to send observers is still under discussion. Last year, Cardinal Tardini pointed out that in Rome too the whole matter was being carefully examined.

2. *Particular attitudes*

Lutheran theologians adhere to the conception of the Church of the "Confession of Augsburg", according to which life together with Christ, which is what ensures the unity of the Church, is found where the Gospel is preached in its purity and the sacraments administered as instituted. On the basis of this Confession it is possible to bring about a Christian world-Church in the full corporative sense. It suffices that each Christian community be united to Christ through word and sacraments in the Holy Spirit. When this is realized, the multiplicity of Churches does not rule out their overriding unity, for each Church represents the body of Christ. The Church's external ordering is not necessary for salvation, and the question of a single Church as a visible institution is wrongly posed. To admit that a definite external unity of the Church was laid down by the Lord and evidenced by the New Testament would

---

[9]These remarks were made in May, 1960. Cf. *Herder-Korrespondenz*, 1960, p. 412.

be to discard Luther and Melanchthon and their entire theology. The Lutheran bishop, Dr. Hanns Lilje, at a session of the "Faith and Order" group of the World Council of Churches in Berlin, stated: "We reject the idea that the Church needs the kind of historical continuity that is apparent in the apostolic succession of bishops. Even if we admit that this idea has a traditional value for individual Churches and Christians, we cannot accept the claim that the historical episcopate is an essential and indispensable element in the ordering of salvation".[10]

In similar terms other leading Lutheran theologians objected to the proposal from the Anglicans and Orthodox to look for a way to full unity by starting from the apostolic succession of bishops.

Calvinist theologians like Emil Brunner go much further than Lutheran in the questions of Institution, Church law and worship. They say that the unity of the Church on earth is something invisible brought about by the Holy Spirit, and that it cannot be established in any historical experience. Anyone who comes through the Word to belief in Christ participates in this inner principle of unity, for the unity of the Church is based solely on the faith of the justified who respond to God's call in the obedience of faith. Wherever this faith becomes

---

[10]Two quotations from a recent official statement may be given. "To confine the plenitude of authority to those who hold office by the apostolic succession is contrary to the sovereign liberty of the Holy Spirit in the Church and inconsistent with the fragility of her earthly existence" under the cross. "If the episcopal succession is understood as the guarantee of the purity of the apostolic tradition or as the exclusive means for attaining and preserving Church unity, we must reject it". Furthermore, the apostolic succession is given the meaning of a continuance in belief and confession of faith, though a succession of persons in the pastoral office is also admitted—a reassertion of the Lutheran position of the past centuries.

The Catholic teaching is that the apostolic succession of bishops is, by divine ordinance, a necessary means for preserving Church unity, but not the only and "exclusive" one. Pius XII calls the Holy Spirit the invisible principle of Church unity (*Mystici corporis*); Leo XIII taught that the Holy Spirit institutes bishops (*Divinum illud*), and it is the constant teaching of the Church that the Eucharist not only symbolizes, but effects, Church unity, as St Augustine and St Thomas in particular explained.

"event" (Ereignis), there arises Church and Church unity. With this kind of "spiritualism" there often goes an extreme eschatologism which speaks of the "unobjectivity of salvation" and the "unrealizability of the Church", and postpones all prospect of a visible unity of the Church to the second coming of Christ.

It is in its doctrine of the Church that Protestantism contrasts most strongly with Catholicism. The evangelical theologian, Hanns Rückert, says: "The questions about the nature of the Church and her true structure have ever been, if not the most ultimate and profound of those in dispute between the Reformation and Catholicism, certainly the most concrete and tangible; besides, they are so bound up with fundamental disagreements that sooner or later we invariably come up against them".[11]

Yet it should not be thought that the fundamental division lies only in the doctrine of the Church or that this is the point of departure and the root cause of the opposition. It is simply that here the contrast is shown most strikingly. Whether the decisive factor in the separation of Churches was the *"sola"* pronouncements (*sola fide, sola scriptura, sola gratia*) or, as van de Pol holds, the inadequate (from the Catholic point of view) sense of the reality of revelation, it is still a fact that all the sixteenth century attempts at union foundered on the doctrine of the Church, and that today the differences in doctrine are most accentuated on this point.

Thus we cannot expect that an exposition, by the coming Council, of a comprehensive doctrine of the Church based on Scripture and Tradition will bring world-Protestantism nearer to the Catholic Church in the immediate future. On the contrary, its first effect will be to bring out more clearly its difference from the Lutheran and Calvinist doctrines. At the

---

[11]H. Rückert, "Kirche und Amt in der evangelischen Theologie" in: *Theologie heute*, Munich, 1960, pp. 108-109.

Reformation it was not moral and other abuses in the Catholic Church that were responsible for the separation, but the new reformed ideas on theological anthropology, faith, God's work of salvation and particularly the Church. The reformers considered the Church with its hierarchical structure, its infallible teaching office of Councils and Popes, with the apostolic succession of bishops by divine ordinance, as contrary to Scripture and so "antichristian". It is true that later exegesis, along with research into the ancient Church and its earliest post-scriptural witness, has undermined many of the exegetical positions of the reformers and altered their picture of the *ecclesia primitiva*. Nonetheless, it is possible for Hermann Volk to state : "Reformed Christianity refuses to be united with Roman Catholic Christianity, for many evangelical Christians continue to hold the Catholic Church as the Church of antichrist. This is a sign that the abuses in the Church at the time of the Reformation were simply the occasion, not the cause, of the separation. Indeed, I have heard it said that the Catholic Church is today more than ever the Church of antichrist, and that not because it has rooted out those abuses to a great extent, but because it has a false conception of itself. It is precisely where it acts according to its specific nature that it is most false, for its understanding of Christian reality is false, and therefore also its understanding of itself".[12]

Despite, or rather on account of, this an exposition by the Council of the doctrine of the Church which answers the questions put by the Reformation out of the fullness of Scripture and Tradition will serve the ultimate goal of reunion. Möhler was right in saying that any really serious theological

---

[12]In a lecture at Münster, 1960. To-day the antichrist idea is held only by way of reversion to the sixteenth century controversies. Maurer considers Luther inherited the antichrist idea as a "dangerous legacy" from the late Middle Ages, and at first applied it " only hesitantly" to the papacy. It was adopted in the schmalkaldic articles, and was based on the false assumption that the papacy "set its authority above the word of God".

attempt in the way of reunion is only possible in so far as the existing disagreement on doctrine is recognized and brought out in all its range and depth.

Evangelical theology has come to pay special attention to the questions of the function, the apostolic succession, the visibility of the Church and its organized unity; and this is something new and bound up with the actual historical situation of the evangelical Church in Germany. The idealistic conception of a purely inward and "platonically" spiritual Church, with the depreciation of its historical form, is now recognized as erroneous and a false interpretation of the Lutheran distinction between outer and inner, spiritual and corporeal, real and unreal Church. Religious individualism, the fruit of the idealistic conception of "Culture-protestantism", is now generally rejected and there is more emphasis on the aspect of community. It is seen that the Church, not the State, is reponsible for its own organization and structure, and that the very nature of the Church implies certain irrefragable laws for its visible ordering.[13] "The thesis of Rudolf Sohms that the charismatic, or spiritual structure of the Christian Church rules out any formation of a legal system has an ultra-spiritualist tone and needs correction. We may even speak of the formulation, emerging now and then in the discussion, of a *jus divinum*, a divine law; the view that it is the Holy Spirit who creates a body for himself in the visible Church points in the same direction."[14]

In spite of the restriction of the *jus divinum* which Rückert at once goes on to impose, this shows clearly what the real

[13]H. Rückert, *Kirche und Amt, loc. cit.*, p. 111. Cf. G. Hoffmann, "Amt und Gemeinde" in: *Begegnung de Christ, loc. cit.*, pp. 193-210. H. Asmussen, "Das Kirchliche Amt in unserer Generation", in: *Die Katholizität der Kirche*, Stuttgart 1957, pp. 237-308; W. Andersen, "Geistliches Amt", in *Evang. Kirchenlexicon*, Vol. I, pp. 108-111, Göttingen, 1956.

[14]H. Rückert, *ibid.*, p. 111. Cf. H. Schütte, "Wiederentdeckung der Kirche in evangelischer Theologie", in: *Theologie und Glaube*, 1960, pp. 339-358. A comprehensive survey of the ecclesiological question will be found in A. Brandenburg, *Evangelische Christenheit in Deutschland am Vorabend des zweiten Vatikanischen Konzils*, Osnabrück, 1960. Cf. also K. Algermissen, *op. cit.*, pp. 910-913.

problem is. We have every hope that the conversations between Catholic and evangelical theologians will gradually remove the misunderstandings that for centuries have, on both sides, impeded discussions on the foundations of ecclesiology.

Thomas Aquinas expressed and himself applied the principle that, in discussions between people of opposing views, a common basis must be looked for first. In discussions with reformed Christianity that basis is, of course, Scripture. Hence the fundamental importance of exegesis for any exposition of ecclesiology made to promote ultimate reunion.

Important too is what St Thomas says about differences of terminology in discussions between Christians of different communions.[15] It is certain that such differences form today one of the greatest obstacles to a theological understanding in the questions at issue. Since the time of the Reformation these differences, which existed even then, have steadily increased, and as long as people fail to realize that they attach different meanings to the same words they will go on talking at cross-purposes.

In a certain sense, a common basis is also offered by the first three Creeds, which the reformed communities recognize as norms of belief, namely the Apostles' Creed, the Nicene, and the so-called Athanasian Creed, which summarizes the whole doctrine of the Trinity and of Christ. We do not ignore the fact that, for example, the meritorious activity of Christ's human nature is not admitted in Luther's Christology, but yet the definitive Christology of Chalcedon is fundamentally acknowledged.

In addition, the doctrinal decisions of the first four Councils were recognized by the Reformers and taken as norms of belief. Luther, in his *Concerning Councils and Churches* (1539), was concerned to show how his principle of *sola scriptura* was consistent with his conviction that the decisions of Nicea (325),

---

[15]*Contra errores Graecorum*, Prooemium.

Constantinople (381), Ephesus (431) and Chalcedon (451) were norms of belief. His argument was that these Councils simply upheld the teaching of Scripture. This is true enough, and it is also true that, for example, St Athanasius himself asserted that the Nicene definitions were scriptural; still the part played by the apostolic tradition in the formulations of these Councils must not be overlooked. It was in the light of Tradition that the Fathers of the Councils interpreted Scripture. As is well known, the Arians, Nestorians and Monophysites appealed to Scripture and adduced a number of texts in their support. The Fathers of the Councils, for their part, to show that their decisions infallibly interpreted the true meaning of Scripture, appealed to the assistance of the Holy Spirit, who preserved them from error as the authorized successors of the apostles. Luther, however, in reducing the authority of Councils simply to a private judgment which each person must make on the scriptural quality of their decisions, not only disavowed the ancient Church's idea of Councils, but also overlooked the part played by Tradition in the decisions of the first four of them.[16]

In the Church, Scripture and Tradition always go together, and admission of the doctrinal decisions of the first four Councils involves, in some way, a recognition of Tradition. We are glad that, in Protestantism today, the problem of "Scripture and Tradition" is considered in a positive way, and that the opposition of Scripture as the word of God to Tradition as the word of man is recognized as a misrepresentation for controversial purposes, and useless for clarifying the problem.[17] Oscar Cullmann's work on Tradition shows the positive

---

[16]Cf. H. D. Altendorf, "Konzile", in: RGG, Vol. 3, col. 1803.

[17]H. Rückert, Schrift-Tradition-Kirche, Lüneberg 1951, pp. 22-23. An excellent survey and commentary on the present position of the discussion of "Tradition und Schrift in der evangelischen und katholischen Theologie der Gegenwart" is given by P. Lengsfeld, Uberlieferung, Paderborn, 1960, pp. 71-213. Cf. also H. Bacht, "Tradition und Lehramt in der ausserkatholischen Kritik am Assumpta-Dogma", in: Die mündliche Uberlieferung, Munich, 1957, pp. 1-62.

results of this new attitude but also its limitations. It also shows a firm adherence in principle to *scriptura sola,* which maintaining that the very composition of the canons of the ancient Church proclaimed it as the sole norm of belief.

Recent Protestant exegesis has discovered "early Catholic elements" in Scripture, and this will facilitate interconfessional discussion on the scriptural basis of the Catholic idea of the Church. But we must not ignore the difficulties of a proof from scripture that will convince those separated from us. They are difficulties arising not only from the special hermeneutic presuppositions of modern Protestant exegetes, but from the special nature of the scriptural exposition of the reformers and of their statements of belief. We have only to think of how Luther called the epistle of St James an "epistle of straw" in comparison with the epistle to the Romans, making his principle of exegesis "what imparts Christ", and how he considered his new conception of justification to be the summary of "what imparts Christ", and the very essence of the Gospel, by which all Scripture is to be assessed. In contrast with this, Calvin's conception of scriptural inspiration is closer to the Catholic.

Over and above this comes the question of whom we are really dealing with as regards all we do to prepare a future reunion. The lack of any teaching authority, the numerous theological opinions at variance with one another, the influx of philosophical concepts and current ideas which threaten to dissolve away whatever Christian substance remains, all this has a bewildering effect on the Catholic observer, so that he has no idea whom he ought to approach as a possible partner in a dialogue. Yet we ought to be aware that, with all their variations, there is a permanent basic tendency in the reformation outlook of the Lutheran, Calvinist and Anglican communities. "We would be absolutely mistaken, were we to overlook this. The statements of belief, especially the *Confessio*

Augustana, Luther's Great and Small Catechisms and such writings have great significance, are even standard works, for many evangelical Christians."[18] Even today in Lutheran communities the minister at his ordination is obliged to adhere to the official statements of belief, and they are the norm which directs the development of doctrine. No doubt, the statements of belief are only *norma normata,* whereas Scripture is *norma normans,* but, on the other hand, Scripture is interpreted on the assumption that the statements of belief contain the *summa scripturae.* However much individual elements of the statements of belief and their exegetical basis have been abandoned, still their general tendency and fundamental attitude remains in some way the starting-point and the pointer of the theology of the reformed Churches and even more so of their parochial life and devotional practice.[19] Moreover the reformed Churches outside Germany, which developed further than those in Germany, are definitely "Confession-Churches", and the various

---

[18]H. Volk, *op. cit.,* p. 7.

[19]E. Schlink, *Theologie der lutherischen Bekenntnisschriften,* Munich 1947, pp.50-55 : "Being a Summa of Holy Scripture, the Confession is to be accepted obligatorily as the model of all Church teaching." Ernst Kinder, "Die lutherische Kirche", in : *Und ihr Netz zerriss,* Stuttgart, 1957, p. 219, says : "No other Church is so explicitly a Confession-Church as the Lutheran. It points to the contents of its Confessions (*Bekenntnisschriften*) as the decisive indication of what it stands for, and these provide the best means for understanding its special nature. It is only from the content of the Confessions, which claim to exhibit the 'centre and Summa' of Holy Scripture as the norm of preaching, that we can define the special character of the Lutheran Church." The reformed Confessions do not have the same significance for the reformed communities of Germany as the Lutheran ones do for the evangelical-lutheran communities. The former communities have neither a Book of Concord nor a Formula of Concord, and their collection of reformed Confessions is not fixed and exclusive either in principle or historically speaking. Paul Jakobs, *Die reformierte Kirche,* p. 293, says : "The Heidelberg Catechism is not to be taken as containing either the concentrated teaching or the kernel of Holy Scripture, and so is not to be put on a level with it or subordinated to it as having the force of ecclesiastical tradition. Its only function, in fact, is to introduce the reader to Scripture." Nonetheless, there is taking place in the reformed Churches a return to the Confessions and a rethinking of them like what is happening in the Lutheran Church. One of the signs of this is Paul Jakobs's publication, *Theologie reformierter Bekenntnisschriften in Grundzügen,*" Neukirchen, Krs. Moers 1959.

statements of belief (*Confessio Belgica*, the Westminster Confession, etc.) have a like normative significance.

The preparatory work for the Council will have to take into account these basic elements of reformed belief and practice, not however looking on them historically as laid down in documents of the Reformation period, but in their various subsequent ramifications and their abiding tendencies. Thus a knowledge of modern Protestant theology is necessary, making us aware how a great number of Protestant theologians reduce the "Confessions" of the Reformation period to certain early-reformation tendencies.

The setting up of a particular "Secretariat for the furtherance of Christian unity" emphasizes the Pope's intention that the preparatory work should look to the possibilities of a future reunion, answering questions put by those outside and concerning itself with their interests. Cardinal Lercaro, the archbishop of Bologna stated, in September 1960, that the Council would not be a "Council for unification" as were those of Lyons and Florence, but a "Council of unity", which, in the spirit of the charity of Christ, would create or strengthen the prerequisites for a better understanding and drawing together of those outside. Though the Catholic Church may admit no compromise on revealed truth, she is prepared in matters of worship and discipline to consider the desires and traditions of the Churches which seek unity.[20]

It is important to emphasize fully that the Council is not called for the purpose of achieving reunion, but for internal matters of the Church. The future of the efforts for union lies in God's hands, and we have to guard against making forecasts or expecting visible results in the near future.

---

[20]*Osservatore Romano*, 16th September, 1960, p. 2.

V

The Attitude of the World Council of Churches

The attitude of the separated Christian communities to the Council can be seen from a resolution proposed by the executive committee of the World Council of Churches to its central committee at its session in St Andrews. The General Secretary, Dr. Visser't Hooft, in his account of the proceedings, warned against "viewing the World Council as a counterpoise to Rome or looking on both as engaged in a struggle for power in the sphere of ecclesiastical politics. The World Council does not aim at ending the separation into many small groups so as to substitute for them larger, but fewer groups. It declines to treat any Church or group of Churches as opponents, but its object is the unity of all who acknowledge Jesus Christ as God and Redeemer."[21]

The resolution of the executive committee on relations with the Roman Catholic Church puts forward the following points :

1. The fact that discussions with the Roman Catholic Church are made possible is to be welcomed.

2. Yet it is to be hoped that the unofficial conversations that have been held between Roman Catholic theologians and other Churches will not be entirely supplanted by official conversations, for at present these informal contacts are most suited to remove misunderstandings.

3. The constitution of the World Council of Churches does not enable it to speak or act for its member Churches in

---

[21]*Evang. Presse-Dienst* (EPD), no. 187, 16th August, 1960. Cf. KNA no. 184, 18th August, 1958.

questions of Church union. In this field each Church makes its own decision in complete freedom. For this reason, the question now at issue, whether the World Council intends to hold conversations, formal or informal, with the Roman Catholic Church on the question of Church unity, is to be answered with a definite "No".

4. Nonetheless, the World Council may use the opportunities that arise to acquaint the Roman "secretariat for the furtherance of Christian unity" with certain fundamental convictions ratified by the plenary assembly or the central committee.

5. The Vatican decision to set up a secretariat to promote connections with the non-Roman Catholic Churches does not mean that the fundamental differences between the two sides have been overcome. All the more reason is there to seize the opportunities for discussion where, at any rate, the real problems will come into the foreground. The part of the World Council in this discussion will be "to set forth the perceptions given us by God in the fifty years since the foundation of our movement".

We ought to welcome this frank and realistic attitude of the World Council of Churches to the problem of union. It shows once again how the question of the nature of Church unity is the real core of theological controversy and interconfessional discussion. The answer to this question depends so closely on the idea formed of the essence of the Church that we may well say the correct response to the question of the unity of the Church is ecclesiology *in actu*.

For this reason, the "Catholic Conference for ecumenical questions" placed the problem of Christian unity in relation to the legitimate differences consistent with this unity in the centre of its discussions held in September 1960 at Gazzada, near Milan. "The examination of past history, the rediscoveries, the deepened perceptions, which all point in one direction, are now so fundamental that they may be looked upon as a wholly new intervention of God's mercy, and no one has the right to prescribe any limits to their range and significance."[22]

According to a recent report from Nyborg (October, 1960), "The General Secretary of the World Council of Churches, Dr. Visser't Hooft (Geneva), told representatives of the Press at the Conference of European Churches in Nyborg that the relations between the World Council and the Roman Catholic Church had again become 'very peaceful'. The appointment by the Pope of Mgr. Willebrands as president of the newly formed secretariat for the union of Christians, in view of the coming Vatican Council, would greatly ease interconfessional discussions; for Mgr. Willebrands knows the World Council almost better than anyone else on the Catholic side. Dr. Visser't Hooft thinks that, even before the next meeting of the World Council, which will bring together, at the end of 1961, Protestant, Anglican and Orthodox Churches in New Delhi, theologians from these and the Roman Catholic Church will meet in greater number for discussions. That will make up for the interruption of the theological talks on unity held the previous year after the summer session of the World Council of Churches at Rhodes."[23]

The strength of the ecumenical movement, overcoming all obstacles to the formation of the World Council of Churches, ultimately derives from an intense desire for Church unity. When we think how young this movement is and how different are the Protestant bodies that belong to it, we begin to realize both the internal difficulties of the World Council and the wonderful achievement of the community already attained. All the same, the outstanding difficulties are great; they are rooted in different conceptions of the Church, and these show

[22]Yves Congar, "Geschichtliche Betrachtungen über Glaubensspaltung und Einheitsproblematik", in *Begegnung der Christen*, Frankfurt, 1959.
[23]*EPD*, 6th October, 1960.

themselves in different views on Church unity. The views of the Orthodox Churches are the closest to Catholic teaching on the unity of the Church as most recently expressed by the Pope in *Ad Petri Cathedram*. What then is the situation of the denominations which arose out of the Reformation?

The Reformation of the sixteenth century deliberately cut itself off from the Roman Catholic Church, without desiring to leave the Church of Christ. The reformed communities, in the process of separation, gave up so many elements of visible unity in the Church's structure, sacraments and life that subsequent history brought further splitting up among Protestants and a number of new denominations. Now the reformed communities are making strenuous efforts to overcome this internal crisis, but this by no means implies that they seek to return to the Roman Catholic Church. In no sense, either historical or ecclesiological, are they contemplating a return to the "father's house" left by their forebears. They want to return neither to the Roman Church of the sixteenth century nor to their own starting-point at the time of the Reformation, the historical forms of which they would like to forego in obedience to the one Lord of the Church. At the same time, the unity they see realized in the Roman Catholic Church is something alien to them, both in the historical and the ecclesiological sense.[24]

---

[24]Cf. the account of the search for unity in G. Hoffmann, *Die ökumenische Bewegung des Weltprotestantismus*, Cologne, 1959, pp. 30-53. See also Ruth Rouse and Stephen Charles Neill, *History of the ecumenical Movement* . . . also Thomas Sartory, *Die ökumenische Bewegung und die Einheit der Kirche, Ein Betrag im Dienste einer ökumenischen Theologie*, Meitingen, 1955, pp. 52-76, 87-201; J. P. Michael, *Christen suchen eine Kirche*, Freiburg, 1958. The attitude of the 53rd General Assembly of the Evangelical Union held in Dusseldorf in September 1960 is expressed in the following statement: "With regard to the efforts of the Catholic Church to re-establish the unity of Christians under Catholic terms, the Evangelical Union sees its chief duty to lie in calling upon the evangelical strength in the personal interpretation of the Gospels and the heritage of the reformation". The President of the Union, Professor Dr. Heinrich Bornkamm, said in his address, that the Fourth Yearbook of the Evangelical Union, which is to be published shortly, would include a discussion on the lines that "the Vatican's constant plea to the 'separated Churches' to return to Rome does not point the way to Christian Unity. So

All they are prepared to do is to make contact with this Church and to recognize their relation to it as an essential problem of the ecumenical movement. Most ecumenical theologians of the reformed confessions are at pains to keep an openness of mind that will make such contact fruitful and will recognize the value of that Church's Christian witness. This attitude of mind on both sides, and applying to both learning and life, is a condition highly favourable to a continuance of theological discussions, whether on the private or official level. The establishment of a Roman secretariat for Christian unity should not restrain, but rather encourage, the private initiative of theologians.

The Church's inner essence and structure is rooted in Christology, and so it is highly significant that a revision has been made of the basic article of the constitution of the World Council of Churches. In its conference at Amsterdam it had adopted the following form : "The World Council of Churches is a community of Churches which acknowledge our Lord Jesus Christ as God and Redeemer." This was judged insufficient by the Orthodox especially, since the Christology of the World Council did not proceed from the doctrine of God made man, and was not in line with the pronouncements of the early Councils, particularly that of Chalcedon.[25] The Anglican

---

long as this deep division in belief exists between the denominations, and Rome upholds her primacy and claim to infallibility, then there can be no question of an organized reunion of the Churches". In the meantime we have only the short abstract of the address to go on, which was given in *Kath. Nachrichten-Agentur* 1st October, 1960 and in *EPD* 23rd-28th September, 1960.

[25]See the message of the Metropolitan Irenaeus of Samos to the Greek Holy Synod in its official organ "Ecclesia" of January, 1957: "The formula 'faith in Christ as God and Redeemer' must be completed by the addition of 'faith in the Holy Trinity'. The current dogmatic basis of the World Council of Churches was, at the time, adopted so as to admit those who denied the Trinity (Quakers, Mennonites, Baptists, Salvationists, etc.). But Antitrinitarians necessarily deny also the divine nature of Christ, or, at any rate, do not regard it as a divine reality in the sense of the Creeds of the first General Councils. The first and fourth Councils with their definition of the dogma of Christ's divinity and humanity are of the highest and universal significance, for human history is based on Christ as God and man; it is because of this that

theologian, Oliver Tomkins, had observed that the Amsterdam formula was capable of very different interpretations. In view of a proposal from the Norwegian Church, made as far back as 1954, and to meet the repeated wishes of the Orthodox, the Central Committee, meeting at St Andrews, resolved to submit a new formula to the plenary assembly at New Delhi in 1961. It was as follows: "The World Council of Churches is a community of Churches which confess the Lord Jesus Christ as God and Redeemer in accordance with Holy Scripture, and therefore strive to fulfil their common vocation to the glory of the Father, Son and Holy Spirit."

The new, extended version mentions Scripture, but not the early Councils, confessing Christ's divinity and redemption according to Holy Scripture. The trinitarian formula is used explicitly, and reference made to the Christian confession of God as Trinity. The Central Committee has declared that the new version is not to be taken as either a "creed" or a comprehensive expression of the Christian faith. Neither does it signify any fundamental alteration of the basis hitherto accepted, but only expresses in scriptural language what binds and holds together the Christian communities of the World Council. Nonetheless, we may say that the revised formula somewhat clarifies the christological basis, which can be understood in the sense of Nicea and Chalcedon. St Athanasius always insisted on the scriptural basis of the Nicean definitions, and the Council of Chalcedon claimed the same for its own. It is true that many Protestant denominations, by reason of their divergent interpretations of Scripture, may press for a different interpretation of the formula; but, on the whole, we welcome the

Christianity has always been a religion of redemption and liberty, one illumined by divine grace communicated in forms and figures taken from the more advanced cultures of various people". The Metropolitan Panteleimon of Salonika, however, held that, in the meaning of the World Council, faith in Christ as God and Redeemer included faith in the Trinity; but the episcopal synod in the end endorsed the view of Irenaeus.

advance made in clarifying the christological basis of the Council.

VI

The Work of the Holy Spirit

On 14th November, 1960, the Pope solemnly opened the preliminaries of the Second Vatican Council in St Peter's, in the presence of the presidents, members and consultors of all the Commissions and of both secretariats. In his address he urged them to examine the procedure and conclusions of the twenty Ecumenical Councils and to use them in their work of preparing the new Council. After mentioning the Council of the Apostles in Jerusalem, he alluded to those of Nicea, Ephesus and Chalcedon, with their increasingly clear and comprehensive development of the dogmas concerning the Trinity and Christ, and finally spoke of the last two Councils. He said that "in the sixteenth century the whole constitution of the Church had been questioned" by the reformers, and that the Fathers of Trent had answered clearly, on the basis of Scripture and Tradition, questions on faith and worship, and sacraments and the reform of morals. Finally, the Vatican Council had "in the short time allowed it set forth clearly the divine constitution of the Church, particularly in regard to the infallibility of the pope in matters of faith and morals."

It may be highly significant that the Pope speaks of the work of the future Council while alluding to the subjects discussed in the two preceding ones, whose treatment of them could not be completed on account of prevailing conditions. "It is clear," he said, "that the preparatory stage demands much time, prolonged patience in the work, and the practice of that love which is accompanied with the better gifts enumerated by St Paul in the thirteenth chapter of the first epistle to the Corinthians. The experience of our own times, along with those of Trent and the First Vatican Council, will serve to indicate the direction of the proposals, discussions and decisions of the forthcoming Council."[26]

In this book we have tried to show how the continuance of the work of the two preceding Councils would be to follow closely the tradition of all past Councils. If the preparatory work of the Council continues this precedent, that would be the most desirable result of the historical research into the earlier Councils so strongly urged by the Pope on the Commissions and secretariats.

The Pope expects great things from the forthcoming Council. He insists that its success depends on the work of the Holy Spirit, who bestows on the Fathers "the best gifts of grace till they shall have finished their work and everything is prepared and set in order for a sublimer stage of knowledge, feeling and vision of the supernatural, that the Spirit of the Lord may descend to glorify and spread love for Jesus Christ, the founder of his holy and glorious Church."[27]

Finally, the Pope quotes the words of the Book of Wisdom which begin the Introit for the Mass of the Holy Spirit: "The Spirit of the Lord hath filled the whole world, and that which containeth all things hath knowledge of the voice" (Wis. 1 : 7).

The meeting of a General Council is not only an act of jurisdiction or of the teaching office, but a liturgical function. Consequently, it always begins with prayer to the Holy Spirit, who alone can bring it to fruition.

The announcement of a future Council has raised high hopes in the whole of Christendom, and caused the longing for unity to be shown more strongly than ever before. We hope and pray

---

[26]*Osservatore Romano*, 14th November, 1960, p. 2.
[27]*ibid.*

that the Holy Spirit of God will make the members of the Commissions keenly alive to the need of men and the duties incumbent on the present time—*vox temporis, vox Dei*—so that the hopes of Christendom may be fulfilled and the longing for unity brought nearer to the end willed by God.

At the conclusion of Vespers in St Peter's on Whit Sunday 1960, the Pope prayed to the Holy Ghost for the preparation of the Council. He turned to the Mother of the divine Word, who is always with us in our prayers, that the Holy Spirit might pour out his gifts on the life of the Church. He recalled the great saints of the eastern Church, Gregory of Nazianzen and John Chrysostom, whose bodies lay in St Peter's. He besought them both to raise up their voices in earnest entreaty for the return of the eastern Churches to the embrace of the one, holy, catholic and apostolic Church. "What a wonderful thing, what flowering of human and divine love, would be the resolve to initiate the reunion of our separated brethren of East and West in the one flock of Christ, the eternal Shepherd! That would be one of the most precious fruits of the Second Vatican Council to the glory of the Lord in heaven and on earth, to universal rejoicing in the plenitude of the mystery of the Communion of Saints."[28]

The highest aim of the Church, to which the ecumenical Council should contribute, said the Pope, is the triumph of Jesus Christ, and he expressed the wish that these words should shine forth over the entrance to the Council as *leitmotiv* of its work: "Doing the truth in charity, we may in all things grow up in him who is the Head, even Christ; from whom the whole body, being compacted and fitly joined together, by what every joint supplieth, according to the operation in the measure of every part, maketh increase of the body, unto the edifying of itself in charity" (Eph. 4 : 15-16).

---

[28]*Osservatore Romano*, 6th June, 1960, p. 2.

EC 7*

The universal longing for unity throughout Christendom is the work of the Holy Spirit, who by his invisible grace draws all to the fullness of the body of Christ in the unity of the Church. However clearly we realize and assess the obstacles to reunion, we must never merely resign ourselves to them. There is a saying of St Ambrose[29] which is repeated often in the medieval *Summae Theologicae* and in instructions on the Christian life—*nescit tarda molimina Sancti Spiritus gratia.* The grace of the Holy Spirit is well able to overcome all doubts and obstacles on the way to unity.

Knowing then that the unity of Christians is not the work of human prudence and organizational ability, but is a gift of God's grace, we turn in faith and confidence in prayer to the Paraclete, the soul of the mystical body, the Church, and the deepest principle of its unity. Pope John has urged both Catholics and their separated brethren to pray constantly for the success of the Council.[30] Let us then raise up our hearts and pray the Holy Spirit to pour out the fullness of his gifts in a new pentecostal stream on the Council and on all who prepare and take part in it and who pray for its success.

---

[29] *In Luc.-Evang.*, Bk. II, Ch. 1.
[30] e.g. in *Ad Petri Cathedram*; cf. also his address of 11th September, 1960, published in *Osservatore Romano* 15th September, 1960; his "Prayer for the ecumenical Council" of 23rd September, 1960; his letter to the Cardinal Vicar of Rome on 28th September, 1960, published in *Osservatore Romano,* 30th September, 1960.

Abbreviations

AAS	Acta Apostolicae Sedis
CJC	Codex Juris Canonici
DAFC	Dictionnaire d'Apologétique et de la Foi Catholique
Denz.	Denzinger-Bannwart, Enchiridion Symbolorum
EPD	Evang. Presse-Dienst (Evangelical News Service)
KNA	Kath. Nachrichten-Agentur
L TH K	Lexikon für Theologie und Kirche
MGH	Monumenta Germaniae Historica
RAC	Reallerikon für die Antike und Christentum
RGG	Die Religion in Geschichte und Gegenwart

Index

Abrecht, P. 110n
Africa—and Christianity 100-2, 117-8, 126-7
Alexander II, Pope 19, 24, 33
Alfonso of Castile 28
Algermissen, K. 150n, 169n
Alivisatos, H. 152n
Altendorf, H. D. 53n, 163-4, 171n
Alzog 140
Ambrose, St. 92, 184
Amsterdam, World Council of Churches Conference 109, 179-80
Anacletus, II, Anti-Pope 18
Andersen, W. 169n
André, R. 104n, 118n
Andrewes, Lancelot 155
Anglicans—and the Second Vatican Council vii, 161-2
Anglicanism—see under Church of England
Antioch, Judaes—Gentile dispute xiv-xv
Antioch, Synods at xvi, xvii, 11n
Arianism xivn, xvii, 1, 87, 171
Aristotelianism 24
Arles, Council of xvi, xvii
Asia — and Christianity 100-2, 117-8, 126-7
Asmussen, H. 169n
Assumption, of Our Lady 75
Athanasius, St. 10, 11, 171, 180

Athenagoras, I (of Constantinople) 150-2, 159
Athenagoras, of Thyatira 152
Aubert, R. 74n, 111n
Augsburg, Peace of 55
Augsburg, Confession of 144, 165, 172-3
Augustine, St. 5, 92, 100, 127, 166n
Avignon, exile of 29

Baar, A. van den 15n
Bacci, Cardinal 146n
Bacht, H. 92n, 171n
Basle, 'Council' of 37, 38, 40
Bea, Cardinal 142-3
Bellarmine, St. Robert 58, 144
Berengarius of Tours 20
Bessarion, Cardinal 40, 42
Betti, U. 74n
Bilio, Cardinal 66
Bishops, Apostolic succesion of 88-90, 115, 166n
Bishops in relation to the pope 68-75, 83-85, 135
Bismarck, 72n
Bizarri, Cardinal 139
Bläser, P. 109n
Boleyn, Anne 153
Boniface, VIII, Pope 28-29, 35, 65
Bornkamm, H. 178n

187

188